The
Garden
Problem
Solver

The Garden Problem Solver

101 SOLUTIONS TO COMMON LANDSCAPING PROBLEMS

CATRIONA TUDOR ERLER
photographs by Jerry Pavia

A ROUNDTABLE PRESS BOOK

SIMON & SCHUSTER
New York London Toronto
Sidney Tokyo Singapore

SIMON & SCHUSTER
Simon & Schuster Building
Rockefeller Center
1230 Avenue of the Americas
New York, New York 10020

A Roundtable Press Book

Directors: Marsha Melnick,
Susan E. Meyer
Project Editor: Marisa Bulzone
Editor: Anne Halpin
Design: Charles Kreloff
Layout: Binns & Lubin/Betty Binns
Cover Design: Charles Kreloff
Color Separations: Oceanic
Graphic Printing, Inc.
Printed in Hong Kong

**Library of Congress
Cataloging-in-Publication Data**
Erler, Catriona T.
  The garden problem solver: 101 solutions to
common landscaping problems/by Catriona
Tudor Erler; photographs by Jerry Pavia.
     p.   cm.
  "A Roundtable Press book" — T.p. verso.
  ISBN 0-671-79804-9
  1. Landscape gardening. 2. Landscape gar-
dening—Pictorial works.
I. Title.
SB473.E754 1994   93–19048
635.9'5—dc20   CIP

To James W. Erler
C.T.E.

Author's Acknowledgments

I would like to thank Peter J. Murray, a landscape designer for Hidden Lane Landscaping & Nursery in Oakton, Virginia, for his help in selecting plants for the plant lists. My heartfelt appreciation is expressed to my editor, Anne Halpin, for her superb work on the manuscript for this book. Thank you also to Linda Teague, who gave Jerry Pavia a full-day's tour of San Diego's outstanding private gardens; and to Pat Welsh, who first introduced me to the world of garden writing and was so generous with her knowledge.

Photographer's Acknowledgments

I would like to thank Marsha Melnick and Susan Meyer for selecting me for this project, and for their efforts to ensure that I got the right photos. I would also like to thank Catriona Tudor Erler for her generosity in sharing photographic prospects and for her enthusiasm with the results. The photographs for a garden book can't be completed without visiting gardens. Over the years I have been fortunate to view some of America's finest public and private gardens with the help given me by private gardeners, garden designers, and landscape architects. I thank you all.

The following people were most helpful in allowing me to visit their garden or leading me to new contacts. Without their kindness, these photographs wouldn't have been possible. Judy Adler, Mr. and Mrs. Aliota, Sydney Baumgartner, Bayberry Nursery, Doug Bayley, Dr. Geoff Beasley, Loie Benedict, Berkeley Botanic Garden, Sam Bibler, Lynn Blackman, Kurt Bluemel, David and Meeche Bodner, Ruth Borun, Mr. and Mrs. Brewer, Christi and Don Brigham, Joan and Joel Brink, John Brookes, Mr. and Mrs. Bryant, Butchart Gardens, Porter Carswell, Cascade Gardens, Chanticleer, Mr. and Mrs. Coster, Connie Cross, Hugh and Mary Palmer Dargan, Roy Davidson, Eve Davis, Mr. and Mrs. Dennis, Denmans, Mary Rose Duffield, Susan Dulaney, The Garden at Elk Rock, Lenore Elvington, Linda Engstrum, Ryan Gainey, Keith Geller, Mr. and Mrs. Giles, Mr. and Mrs. Glen, Isabel Green, the late Bill Gunther, Levans Hall, Mr. and Mrs. Hall, Mr. and Mrs. Ham, Harland Hand, Virginia Hays, Mrs. Hendricks, Herb Farm, Mr. and Mrs. Don Hewitt, Alex Hill, Dan Hinkley, Jody Honnen, Mr. and Mrs. Horsey, Angie and Alice Hundera, Norman Johnson, Mr. and Mrs. Kistler, Mr. and Mrs. Koehler, Kurisu International, Leach Botanical Garden, Mr. and Mrs. Lind, Lotusland, Ron Lutsko, Manito Park, Patty McGee, Meadowbrook Farms, Mrs. Monk, Chole Morgan, Robert Murase, Mr. and Mrs. Murdoch, Peter Newton, Oehme and Van Sweden, Old Westbury Gardens, Vera Peck, Mr. and Mrs. Peterson, George Radford, Roger Raiche, Rancho Los Alamitos, Tich and Michael Rehill, Joan Roberts, Rocky Dale Gardens, Mr. and Mrs. Rosenberg, Chris Rosmini, Wesley Rouse, Joe and Gloria Sacco, Santa Barbara Water Gardens, Steve Schramm, Michael Schultz, Stephanie Schutley, David Seeler, Mr. and Mrs. Severence, Frances Shannon, Bill Slater, Anne Smith, Cecil and Molly Smith, Mrs. C. Lindsay Smith, Lisa Stamm, Mr. and Mrs. Stanley, Phyllis Stephens, Daniel Stewart, Strybing Arboretum, Linda Teague, Sir John Thuoron, Mrs. Tilt, Tintinhull, Jean Turner, Lawrence Underhill, Mr. and Mrs. Valentine, Van Dusen Botanical Garden, Bob Venuti, Jean Vollum, Jan Walthemath, John Warner, Washington Cathedral Herb Garden, Wayside Gardens, Pat Welsh, Mr. and Mrs. Frank White, Lois Woodall, Lynn Woodbury, Chris Woods, Mr. and Mrs. Zervos, Ngaere Zohn.

Contents

Preface

The famous 18th-century English landscape designer Lancelot "Capability" Brown earned the nickname "Capability" because of his repeated claim that any landscape, no matter how difficult, had "capabilities for improvement." This optimistic attitude is worthy of any homeowner with a plot of land to cultivate. No matter how many problems the space presents, it has capabilities for improvement.

No property is perfect, and all homeowners face challenges in transforming their plot of land into their own little piece of paradise. Along the west coast, for example, hundreds of thousands of building lots are cut into hillsides so that each property has a bare, steep slope rising up to the house or falling off behind it. In the southwest, and increasingly in other parts of the United States, lack of water is a challenge, making it difficult or impossible to maintain lawns and traditional landscape plants without extensive watering. In some parts of the southeast, homeowners face the opposite problem: an excess of standing water that creates bogs. Gardeners everywhere are pressed for space. In most urban and suburban areas, building lots are getting smaller and smaller, providing less and less space for landscaping.

Fortunately, any property, no matter what its limitations, can be beautifully landscaped by those who know how to work with the challenges presented by a particular site. In fact, with creativity and the right landscaping solution, a difficult situation can often be transformed into a wonderful garden asset. A rocky hillside can be turned into an alpine rock garden, while an unwanted stump that's too difficult to remove might become a planter, a garden seat, or a pedestal for a garden table.

This book is designed to spark ideas and inspire creative solutions that will highlight the amazing capabilities of your garden. In an innovative, easy-to-use form, the book describes twelve of the most common landscaping problems, including arid climate, deep shade, steep slopes, and unsightly views, and offers a variety of creative ways to solve them. Each chapter opens with a description of the problem and a rundown of possible ways to deal with it. Specific, detailed solutions follow, most illustrated with photographs of real gardens where the problem has been successfully solved. You can read the entire chapter or skim through the pages, looking for solution headings and photographs that appeal to your taste and budget.

When presented with so many inspiring garden scenes, it is easy to be tempted by an unrealistically large garden renovation. Unless you have unbounded energy, or can afford to hire out most of the labor, you are wise to limit yourself to small sections of the garden at a time. Start with an overall plan, so you know where you are going, but then tackle it in stages. That way, you will be saved the defeating sense of being overwhelmed, and you can enjoy the fulfillment of seeing each part of the plan brought to a satisfactory conclusion. Remember, it takes many years to create a great garden, and even once you have achieved the total look you want, you will probably continue making a little change here and adding a new plant there. That's part of the process and part of the fun.

PROBLEM ONE:

Lack of Water

As population density increases throughout the nation and droughts occur more frequently, water conservation is becoming an important issue everywhere. Xeriscaping, the art of landscaping for dry climates, is the trend of the 1990s, especially in the arid west. As a result, gardeners are learning that a dry landscape doesn't have to be a barren one. The scope and diversity of the available plant materials, particularly plants that use little water, are increasing each year as nurseries respond to the demands of water conservation. Many of these plants are native Americans, which are growing in popularity and availability; others are introductions from South Africa and Australia. To keep up with the demand, hybridizers are hard at work developing new varieties of existing dry-climate plants, and breeding to develop drought tolerance in thirstier species.

Homeowners are removing lawns and replacing them with paved surfaces that add living space to a home, or with lower-maintenance, drought-tolerant ground covers. In general, Americans are becoming more creative when gardening in arid climates, and their gardens are the better for it.

1

Create shade for a cooler microclimate in hot, dry gardens

As Thomas Jefferson wrote, shade is the Elysium of a hot-climate garden. If it isn't available by natural means such as a broad, spreading tree, you can create your own shady retreat. Lath-covered structures are ideal because the slats allow in enough light to grow flowering shade plants, while keeping the space cool and pleasant.

Warm-climate gardeners who want to propagate and grow large quantities of temperate-climate shade plants should consider building a lath house, the sides and roof of which should be constructed of lath strips spaced about 1 to 1½ inches apart. This is the hot-climate substitute for a greenhouse, providing filtered sun for plants such as fuchsias, cymbidiums, and begonias. In addition to serving as a nursery for rooting cuttings, a lath house is an ideal spot to keep flowering plants when they are out of season. If possible, situate the lath house in full sun, and arrange the lath strips to run north and south, so that the shade will shift evenly as the sun moves from east to west. Any lath structure should be built of redwood or pressure-treated wood so that it will stand up to outdoor conditions for years.

Shade a walkway with an arbor covered by vining plants. Here, hanging baskets of impatiens supply plenty of color at eye level throughout the summer when the vines are not in bloom. Other good plants for hanging baskets in the shade are fuchsias, begonias, brunfelsia, ferns, and epiphyllum.

Transform a patio into a bower with a lath roof, hanging baskets, and potted flowers. Plant flowering vines, either in containers or in the ground, to grow up the supports and over the top of the lath structure. In this case, the lath panels closest to the house are removable, so that more light is allowed into the living room during the winter.

2

Plant a desert garden of cacti and succulents

Instead of trying to change nature by planting water-demanding lawns, shrubs, and other conventional horticultural elements in a desert area, create a cultivated garden with indigenous plants.

The most distinctive and recognizable plants native to desert regions are succulents and cacti, all of which are able to store water in their leaves or stems. They come in a wide array of sizes, ranging from the 25-foot-tall saguaro cactus to the tiny lithops, which resemble pebbles more than plants. Some, such as donkey's tail (*Sedum morganianum*), wax plant (*Hoya carnosa*), and Christmas cactus (*Schlumbergera bridgesii*), are ideal for growing in hanging baskets. A few, including some sedum and sempervivum hybrids and the beavertail-like cactus known as prickly pear (*Opuntia*), can survive winters in most parts of the United States.

Use shallow-rooted varieties of cacti and succulents in rock crevices and in pots. Large aloes and cacti such as ocotillo and saguaro make excellent specimen plants. Smaller varieties usually look better planted in clumps or groups. Spreading ice plants, such as *Lampranthus spectabilis*, are popular as ground covers in dry western gardens, but also consider using different succulents, such as *Sedum* X *rubrotinctum*. Another idea is to combine different low-growing succulents in massed groups to create a patchwork effect. Most succulent ground covers require about 80 percent less water than a lawn, making them less labor-intensive and more practical for the environment.

A desert garden of cacti doesn't need to be a barren place. Here, a mass planting of barrel cactus (*Echinocactus grusonii*) flourishes amid a "forest" of organ-pipe cactus (*Lemaireocereus*), creating a mixture of form and color that is pleasing to the eye.

These tall-standing cacti, *Notocactus leninghausii*, resemble soldiers marching in serried ranks, making an impressive display in this desert garden. Generally, a cluster of like cacti look better than one lone plant.

Mass-planted succulents create a fascinating garden with infinite variety of color and texture. Here, hundreds of pearl echeveria (*Echeveria elegans*) carpet the ground, with the pinecone-like *Agave victoriae-reginae* and the spiky *Xanthorrhoea quadrangulata* as striking accents.

3

Mulch the garden to conserve soil moisture

Mulch is one of a gardener's best friends. It helps conserve soil moisture, slows the growth of weeds, keeps plant roots cool on a hot day and warm on a cold one, and, if it is of an organic material, decomposes to add nutrients to the soil.

The variety of mulching materials is diverse. Among the organic possibilities, all are about equally effective. The choice depends then on what kind of mulch you find most aesthetically appealing, and on which material is most economical and easily available in your area. Possibilities include grass clippings (spread in thin layers), straw, bark (in either nuggets or shredded form), cocoa hulls, pine needles (an excellent source of acid for plants such as azaleas), and shredded newspaper (except sections with colored ink).

4.

Create a garden of drought-tolerant native plants

Drought-tolerant native plants are often rejected by home gardeners because they tend to look scrubby in the wild. However, most plants look unkempt if no one cares for them, and many natives can become quite civilized if looked after in a garden. Once established, they generally require little or no watering, and they tend to be free of pests and diseases.

If you live in the Midwest, a prairie garden of hardy deep-rooted plants indigenous to the area is a good choice. Prairie plants have adapted themselves to tolerate the wind, drought, heat, and cold typical of the region.

Californians can choose from the wide variety of plants classed as California natives. Each year brings a host of new choices as burgeoning interest and demand prompt hybridizers to develop new cultivars with longer bloom seasons and greater adaptability. Bear in mind, though, that during their first year, even these drought-tolerant plants need extra care and adequate water to become established in the garden.

Desert environments range from the cold lands of the Great Basin to the searing hot deserts of Arizona, New Mexico, and Texas. In each region, different native plants have adapted to the rigors and extremes of the local climate.

Local boulders, carefully placed by the landscape designer, add character and sculptural interest in this informal, drought-tolerant garden planted with potentilla, monkshood (*Aconitum*), and yarrow.

Drought-tolerant plants

TREES AND SHRUBS

Barberry (*Berberis*), zones 6–9

Bottlebrush (*Callistemon*), zones 8–10

California lilac (*Ceanothus*), zones 8–10

Cotoneaster species, zones 5–9

Cotton lavender (*Santolina chamaecyparissus*), zones 6–9

Crape myrtle (*Lagerstroemia indica*), zones 7–10

Deodar cedar (*Cedrus deodara*), zones 7–9

Elaeagnus, zones 7–9

Eucalyptus, zones 9–10

European olive (*Olea europaea*), zones 9–10

Firethorn (*Pyracantha*), zones 6–10

Flannel flower (*Fremontodendron*), zones 8–10

Ginkgo biloba, zones 5–9

Golden-rain tree (*Koelreuteria paniculata*), zones 6–9

Heavenly bamboo (*Nandina domestica*), zones 7–10

Indian hawthorn (*Rhaphiolepis indica*), zones 8–10

Jacaranda (*Jacaranda mimosifolia*), zone 10

Lantana, zones 9–10

Lavender (*Lavandula*), zones 6–9

Mimosa, or silk tree (*Albizia julibrissin*), zones 1–10

Oleander (*Nerium oleander*), zones 8–10

Pittosporum, zones 8–10

Plumbago auriculata,
zones 9–10

Pride of Madeira (*Echium fastuosum*), zone 10

Poinsettia (*Euphorbia pulcherrima*), zones 9–10

Pomegranate (*Punica*),
zones 8–10

Rock rose (*Cistus*) zones 7–9

Rosemary (*Rosmarinus*),
zones 7–10

Rugosa rose (*Rosa rugosa*),
zones 4–9

St. John's-wort (*Hypericum calycinum*), zones 7–9

Sumac (*Rhus*), zones 3–9

Tamarisk (*Tamarix*), zones 6–9

Yew (*Taxus*), zones 5–7

VINES

Bougainvillea, zone 10

Grape (*Vitis vinifera*), zones 6–9

Silver lace vine (*Polygonum aubertii*), zones 4–9

Trumpet creeper (*Campsis radicans*), zones 5–9

Trumpet honeysuckle (*Lonicera sempervirens*), zones 4–9

Wisteria, zones 4–10

BULBS AND PERENNIALS

Agave, zones 9–10

Aloe, zone 10

Tickseed (*Coreopsis*), zones 4–9

Wormwood (*Artemisia*),
zones 3–10

Yarrow (*Achillea millefolium*),
zones 4–8

5

Conserve water with a drip irrigation system

Experts estimate that a drip irrigation system can cut water usage from 25 to 50 percent, depending on how effectively it is designed and on the dryness of the climate. In a drip system, water is delivered to the plants through slender plastic tubes at a rate as slow as half a gallon per hour. As a result, the water soaks deeply into the soil, going directly to the plants' root systems. A garden can be deep-watered with less frequency, and there is no waste due to runoff and evaporation.

Drip systems offer benefits in addition to water conservation. Since the water is concentrated exactly where it is needed and soaks in deeper because of the slow delivery, plants tend to grow faster and more evenly. Weeds are minimized because the water is directed toward the garden plants; weeds won't grow where there is no water. Because foliage never gets wet, there is less chance of disease and burning, and the need for pesticides, especially on plants such as roses, is reduced. Liquid fertilizers can be added directly through the system, so that the application occurs at a regular pace and is accurately measured.

With normal watering conditions, a plant may go through cycles of being too dry and then too wet. This can cause the plant to undergo stress that is not severe enough to cause visible symptoms, but nonetheless affects growth. You can minimize the stress on plants by delivering optimum amounts of water and fertilizer directly to the roots. This will bring plants to their peak genetic potential.

6

Use drought-tolerant ground covers rather than grass

One wag has remarked that it is cheaper to get a green lawn by spreading dollar bills across the ground than by paying to water, fertilize, and maintain grass. In addition to the monetary expense, you must also consider the high cost in water usage required to maintain a beautiful lawn. Even with heat-resistant, drought-tolerant varieties of lawn grass, it takes hundreds of gallons of water to keep an expanse of grass lush and green. During drought periods in California, some communities have limited water use to 20 gallons a day per person in a household. Expending water to irrigate lawns was not an acceptable option.

Fortunately, there are attractive, drought-tolerant ground covers that make appropriate lawn substitutes in many landscaping situations. You might want to con-

Left: Gazania, a wonderful import from South Africa, makes a dazzling ground cover during peak bloom in late spring to early summer. In mild climates, it will continue to bloom sporadically throughout the year. Best of all, gazania generally needs watering only about twice a month.

Below: Creeping thyme requires infrequent watering in hot zones and can withstand some foot traffic. It gives off a delicious scent when crushed and is also used to flavor food.

sider planting trailing varieties of saltbush (*Atriplex*), euonymus, lantana, African daisy (there are three closely related plants by this name: *Arctotis*, *Dimorphotheca*, and *Osteospermum*), juniper, rosemary, star jasmine (*Trachelospermum*), or germander (*Teucrium*). Also to be listed among the good, drought-tolerant plants for you to try are dichondra, gazania, ivy, and periwinkle (*Vinca*).

7

Create a drought-tolerant flower garden

A drought-tolerant garden doesn't have to be without flowers. A wealth of beautiful flowering plants that require very little water is available, many imported from Australia and South Africa.

Some choices that remain attractive all season (year-round in warm climates) and require little maintenance are daylilies (*Hemerocallis*), agapanthus, African daisies (*Arctotis* hybrids), society garlic (*Tulbaghia violacea*), grevillea, cigar plant (*Cuphea ignea*), and French lavender. For seasonal color, consider penstemon, Transvaal daisy (*Gerbera*), rudbeckia (also called gloriosa daisy or black-eyed Susan), coreopsis, Swan-River daisy (*Brachycome iberidifolia*), iris, bird-of-paradise (*Strelitzia*), and lobelia. Drought-tolerant choices among the spring-flowering bulbs include freesia, ranunculus, leucojum, muscari,

some narcissus, babiana, star of Bethlehem (*Ornithogalum*), ixia, and sparaxis.

Many flowering shrubs are suitable for planting in a flower garden, including, for warm climates, protea, oleander (if kept small), pride of Madeira (*Echium fastuosum*), ceanothus, and bush monkey flower (*Mimulus*). In colder climates, look to rock rose (*Cistus* spp.), Spanish broom (*Genista hispanica*), and mahonia.

The gray, lavender, and soft green tones of santolina, lavender, and rosemary blend harmoniously in this low-maintenance, drought-tolerant hillside garden.

The spiky leaves of New Zealand flax (*Phormium*) provide a backdrop to this colorful display of drought-tolerant flowers. Among the pretty clumps of blooms are the rosy pink globes of sea pink (*Armeria*), lavender-flowered society garlic, yellow African daisies, and rock rose.

8

Create a garden of drought-tolerant shrubs

Far from being boring, a well-planned garden of shrubs can be a gorgeous display of texture, form, and the infinite variety of shades of green.

Gardens composed primarily of shrubs have an august tradition in the garden style of Italy, where shrubs are used extensively to create green garden rooms.

For floral color, select from a wide range of flowering shrubs. Hibiscus is an excellent drought-tolerant choice. In mild climates, some varieties will bloom twelve months of the year. Other shrubs will also provide year-round interest in a variety of ways. For example, the pyracantha bush blooms profusely in spring, then sprouts bright berries well into the fall.

Junipers, holly, and false cypress (*Chamaecyparis*) are masterfully combined in this beautiful garden of shrubs.

9

Create a garden near a swimming pool

Planting gardens around a swimming pool is more challenging than you might expect. Pool water, which has high chlorine levels, may splash into the beds and damage the plants. The standard solution is providing ample decking around the pool and keeping the plantings well away from the edge. A more natural-looking approach is to bring the garden close to the pool, but in raised beds to minimize the risk that chlorinated water will splash onto the plants. Include a good drainage system in the decking around the pool to direct water away from the raised planting beds.

If the addition of raised beds would mean the expensive reconstruction of existing decking, you might invest instead in large pots. Place them around the pool, and fill them to overflowing with flowers or a cycad or small palm to bring height to the space.

The tall ornamental grass *Miscanthus sinensis* 'Morning Light' growing near the edge of this stone-rimmed swimming pool helps relieve the expansive flat plane of water and grass; it also casts attractive reflections on the pool surface. Notice that the beds nearest the pool are raised to keep the plants well away from the chlorinated water. In this instance, the raised beds and tall plant groupings also help screen the pool utility area and the nearby fence.

10

Create a garden with a reflecting pool or pond

Where natural ponds are uncommon, create your own. Since ancient times, gardeners in hot climates have used pools and ponds to provide a cooling effect in their gardens. The design possibilities are limitless, from a tiny pond created in a sealed barrel to a large, shallow reflecting pool filled with waterlilies, waterworks, and sculptures. The ponds may be free-form or geometric in shape, formal or informal, naturalistic or stylistic, depending on your taste, your budget, and what will go best with your house and garden. The goal is to create a design that will provide a refreshing oasis in a parched landscape.

A reflecting pool serves as a planter for reeds, waterlilies, and other aquatic plants, while adding lushness to an otherwise dry environment.

Right: Soften the extensive hardscape of a pool and patio by putting drought-tolerant plants, such as this ivy and geranium combination, around the perimeter of the water.

Far right: The alyssum, kangaroo paw (*Anigozanthos*), and lavender planted around this pool enhance its cleverly designed naturalistic look.

Below: A tiny pond created in the recesses of large boulders adds a special touch to this arid rock garden. Among the drought-tolerant plants here are iris, sea pink (*Armeria*), and echeveria.

11

Create a garden with a recirculating fountain

The sound of splashing water as it falls from a fountain is both soothing to the spirit and cooling to the body. In fact, falling water does cool and humidify the air directly around it, creating a beneficial microclimate for plants that don't thrive in the dry air of much of the Southwest. In a small, enclosed garden save space by building the fountain into a wall or fence, or make it the cool focal point in the center of a courtyard.

Fountain designs range from simple, businesslike sprays and water jets in the middle of a pond to fantastic, ornate creations. Some are whimsical, some are formal and elegant. Others, such as those made of painted tiles, reflect styles borrowed from Spain and Portugal.

This multitiered fountain allows water to fall from several levels, creating a pleasing sound while attracting birds to bathe in its sheltered basin.

Place a fountain near a seating area where you can enjoy the melody played by falling water.

12

Create a garden using gravel or stones as a ground cover

In extremely dry areas where lawns and even drought-tolerant ground covers use too much water, gravel and stones are attractive, inexpensive alternatives to solid paving. The benefits are many. Gravel or stones are relatively easy to install, and trees, shrubs, and even plants can be grown directly in them. When it does rain, they drain rapidly, and on gentle slopes, they help prevent erosion. Avoid laying gravel at the base of a steep slope, however, because soil washing off the hillside will mix with the gravel and spoil its look. To keep the gravel stable, lay it at least 2 inches deep and slightly below the edging or adjacent paving to keep it from scattering.

Above: In a sophisticated varia-
tion on the parterre concept of
creating designs with hedges and
flowers, this gardener used stones
in subtly different shades of gray
to form a graceful "yin and yang"
pattern.

Right: A dry river bed of stone is
a popular feature of Japanese
gardens. Here, it is an ideal solution to the long, narrow space
along the side of the house.

Far right: The arrangement of
gray-white stones creates an
interesting hillside pattern and
stops erosion as well. Drought-
tolerant verbena and a barrel
cactus (*Echinocactus*) planted in
the interstices soften the look.

13

Use hardscape creatively

Although expensive at the outset, in the long run a paved surface, called *hardscape*, is extremely cost-effective. Once it's laid, your expenses are over; in contrast, a lawn requires continual maintenance and outlay. A well-planned hardscape also effectively extends the living space of your home when it forms the floor surface of a usable "garden room."

The choice of materials for paving in the garden has grown enormously in the past few years. New diamond-hard tiles have been developed by re-fusing pulverized granite. Some tiles come in matching indoor and outdoor versions so that people can create a continuity between house and garden spaces. Stone products now are being imported from around the world. Particularly attractive are multicolored slates from China. Concrete, the old standby, now is often tinted for added interest and textured for slip resistance.

A combination of materials, such as this brick and flagstone, helps break the monotony of a large paved area with its interesting design.

The circular pattern of these bricks adds pleasing form and texture to this garden. The rosette design resembles an enormous pink blossom.

These widely tiered steps appear to float above the paving, flowing out from the nearby stream. Hardscape can be an artistic asset to the garden; it need not be a boring expanse of emptiness.

The drought-tolerant feverfew (*Tanacetum parthenium*, formerly *Chrysanthemum parthenium*) growing in the crevices of this stone patio and bench introduces a pleasing living element to the scene.

14

Create a garden with containers and sculpture

In a xeriscape garden, containers offer an opportunity to indulge a yen for water-hungry plants used on a limited scale. You can also use some tricks to increase water retention in containers. Plastic containers hold moisture longer than clay pots. If the look of plastic offends you, or if the dark-colored plastic is getting too hot in the sun and burning the plant's roots, slip the plastic pot into a more attractive clay or ceramic cachepot. Choose an outer pot a few inches bigger than the inside one, and fill the space between them with an insulating layer of sphagnum moss or lightweight mulch. If you water both pots, the evaporating water from the outer pot will help cool the inner one. Also, mulch the soil in the pots to retain moisture, and spray the foliage with an antitranspirant, such as Wilt-Pruf or Cloud Cover, to reduce water evaporation that occurs through the plant's leaves.

Containers planted with flowers soften hard surfaces, add height to a flat environment, and bring color into a garden. When planted with an interestingly shaped shrub or small tree, they become a form of sculpture.

Above: Pots of blooming daffodils transform a bleak stone staircase into a welcoming entryway.

Above right: The minimalist grouping of sculpted pots in this exquisite understated garden is a masterful example of the principle of less is more.

Right: Bring together pots filled with drought-tolerant plants of diverse colors and textures for an attractive composition.

PROBLEM TWO:

Too Much Water

Water adds a magical, enchanting quality to a garden. It is also versatile. Depending on how it is used, water can be peaceful or enlivening, sophisticated or primitive, formal or informal. Perhaps because it is one of the basic elements of life, people usually respond deeply to the presence of water in a garden. If you have an abundance of it, use it to handsome effect.

But water that stands in puddles and saturates soil can cause problems, too. Soil that is poorly drained and constantly soggy can cause root rot, and may suffocate plants not adapted to such conditions. The water forces oxygen out of the soil and, after a time, plant roots will be deprived of that essential element. Unable to fuel the photosynthetic process that nourishes them, the plants will eventually die. When standing water doesn't lend itself to creating pools, streams, or waterworks, consider removing the problem with drains or raised beds or accepting the wet conditions and planting a bog garden.

15

Improve drainage with a raised-bed garden

One straightforward solution to boggy ground is to rise above it. Pile the soil high, and contain it with structured sides made of a material such as wood (old railway ties are an inexpensive option), brick, or stone. If you are raising the bed just 6 or 8 inches, the roots of low-growing border plants or ground covers planted around the edge of the bed will also hold the soil in place, making structured sides unnecessary. In this case, slope the edges instead.

The heights to which you need to go will depend on what you intend to plant. Shallow-rooted plants will manage with 8 inches of soil. Plants with deeper roots may require as much as 2 or 3 feet. Where drainage is very poor, put down a layer of sand or gravel before adding topsoil and manure, and provide drainage out of the bottom of the bed. Also see solution 43 in chapter 5.

A raised bed filled with good topsoil has two distinct benefits: It brings the flowers closer to eye level and solves the problem of too much water collecting because of poor drainage.

16

Install drainage systems or construct berms

Amending the soil or providing raised planting beds is much easier than installing underground drains in your garden. However, if your garden has obvious topographical problems, one or more of the various drainage options may be necessary. Choose the system that is best suited to your specific application. Among the choices are gravel-filled trenches, drain tiles, and flexible plastic drainpipes.

In locations where water is flowing downhill and collecting at a low point, consider building a berm: Design a mound of earth to block the flow of water to the low-lying area, and to direct it away to a convenient disposal spot. Then cover the berm with shrubs and/or perennials. The berm creates a lovely raised planter, and the roots will hold the berm in place, preventing erosion.

17

Construct a boardwalk through the garden

A boardwalk creates the delightful illusion of floating slightly above the garden. Placed over water or marshy ground, it provides access to parts of the property that are otherwise unreachable. A boardwalk also offers an opportunity to view up close particularly choice plants and wildlife that would normally remain remote. These qualities make a stroll along a boardwalk a special experience, somewhat akin to following the yellow brick road; there is a sense of expectation, of discovery, perhaps even an adventure at the end of your journey.

A boardwalk may traverse large expanses of marshy ground, or it may cover a short distance in a home garden. Here, it allows people to walk through the beds of *Iris pseudacorus* growing in the water.

18

Lighten dense clay soil with compost, other organic matter, and sand

Dense clay soil can slow drainage significantly, creating problems during periods of heavy rain. To lighten the soil and aid aeration and drainage, add organic soil amendments. To ease the job of adding amendments to heavy clay, and to protect the soil structure as you work, water the ground thoroughly a few days before you plan to begin digging. The slightly dried, but still-moist, soil should crumble when turned over with a shovel. Before adding amendments, turn the soil with a spade or a large garden fork. Work your way from one end of the garden to the other, digging one row then the next. Dig in as deeply as possible (8 to 10 inches), and turn the soil on its side, rather than upside down. Break up the clods of earth as you go.

A 100-square-foot bed should take about 4 cubic feet of compost and other organic matter (spread 2 to 4 inches deep), and about 10 pounds of complete fertilizer. Spread the additives evenly over the ground, and once again dig and turn the soil, mixing in the amendments thoroughly. Tamp down the uneven ground, and then rake the area to remove all clods and rocks near the surface and to provide a smooth, cultivated growing space. Water again, letting the moisture soak deep into the soil.

Moisture-loving and bog-tolerant plants

TREES AND SHRUBS

Bald cypress (*Taxodium distichum*), zones 5–10

Birch (*Betula*), zones 3–8

Black gum (*Nyssa sylvatica*), zones 5–9

Broad-leaved paperbark (*Melaleuca quinquenervia*), zone 10

Dawn redwood (*Metasequoia glyptostroboides*), zones 5–10

Red swamp maple (*Acer rubrum*), zones 4–9

Sweet bay magnolia (*Magnolia virginiana*), zones 6–9

Willow (*Salix*), zones 4–9

FLOWERING PLANTS

Arrowhead (*Sagittaria latifolia*), zones 5–10

Arum lily (*Zantedeschia aethiopica*), zones 8–10

Astilbe, zones 5–8

Canna hybrids, zones 7–10

Brass Buttons (*Cotula coronopifolia*), zones 7–9

Cuckoo flower (*Cardamine pratensis*), zones 5–8

Garden groundsel (*Ligularia*), zones 4–8

Globeflower (*Trollius*), zones 5–8

Greater spearwort (*Ranunculus lingua*), zones 4–8

Iris species, zones 4–9

Lizard's tail (*Saururus cernuus*), zones 4–9

Marsh marigolds (*Caltha palustris*), zones 4–9

Pickerel weed (*Pontederia cordata*), zones 4–9

Thalia, zones 6–10

Water arum (*Calla palustris*), zones 3–8

Water forget-me-not (*Myosotis scorpioides*), zones 7–9

Water plantain (*Alisma plantago-aquatica*), zones 5–8

Yellow loosestrife (*Lysimachia punctata*), zones 7–9

FOLIAGE PLANTS

Bur reed (*Sparganium erectum*), zones 5–9

Cameleon plant (*Houttuynia cordata* 'Chamaeleon'), zones 5–9

Gunnera, hardiness varies

Dwarf papyrus (*Cyperus haspans*), zones 9–10

Ferns, hardiness varies

Grassy-leaved sweet flag (*Acorus gramineus*), zones 6–10

Hosta, zones 4–9

Taro root (*Colocasia esculenta*), zones 9–10

RUSHES AND REEDS

Bowles' golden sedge (*Carex elata* 'Aurea'), zones 4–8

Cattail (*Typha latifolia*), zones 3–10

Chinese water chestnut (*Eleocharis tuberosa*), zones 7–10

Corkscrew rush (*Juncus Effusus* 'Spiralis'), zones 5–9

Dwarf cattail (*Typha minima*), zones 6–9

Horsetail (*Equisetum hyemale*), zones 3–9

Mist flower (*Eupatorium rugosum*), zones 4–9

Zebra sedge (*Scirpus lacustris* 'Zebrinus'), zones 6–9

19

Create a garden of bog plants

Transform a liability into an asset by turning a muddy spot of standing water into a beautiful bog garden. A large number of plants that can make do in a dry situation, including astilbe and hostas, really prosper when provided with a constant supply of water. Other garden plants that enjoy the extra moisture are Japanese and pseudacorus iris, primulas, lobelias, daylilies, and loosestrife (except the purple variety, which is so invasive that it is destroying wetlands in many areas of the country). See the plant list for less well-known plants that can enhance a bog garden.

A bog garden is delightful beside a garden pool, creating a natural transition between the water garden and the dry land. If your land isn't naturally boggy, you can create the necessary conditions by excavating the soil about 12 inches deep and then lining the hole with heavy plastic. Refill the hole with dirt, and water heavily. Watch for signs of drying out during long periods of hot, dry weather, and add water if necessary.

A bog garden is a wonderfully natural-looking way to make the transition from a garden pond or pool to dry land.

Siberian iris is one of several iris species that thrive in standing water. The flowers, which resemble those of Dutch iris, bloom in late spring in colors spanning the range of blue, purple, red, and white. September and October are the months to divide old clumps that are getting hollow in the center.

Plants for a water garden

American lotus (*Nelumbo lutea*), zones 4–10

Bog bean (*Menyanthes trifoliata*), zones 5–8

Frog's-bit (*Hydrocharis morsus-ranae*), zones 7–10

Golden-club (*Orontium aquaticum*), zones 7–10

Grassy-leaved sweet flag (*Acorus gramineus*), zones 6–9

Jesuit nut, water chestnut (*Trapa natans*), zones 6–10

Myriad leaf (*Myriophyllum verticillatum*), zones 4–10

Parrot's-feather (*Myriophyllum aquaticum*), zones 7–10

Sacred lotus (*Nelumba nucifera*), zones 5–9

Salvinia auriculata, zone 10

Spatterdock, yellow pond lily (*Nuphar lutea*), zones 5–10

Water hawthorn (*Aponogeton distachyos*), zones 9–10

Water hyacinth (*Eichhornia crassipes*), zones 8–10

Water lily (*Nymphaea*), hardiness varies

Water poppy (*Hydrocleys nymphoides*), zones 9–10

Water soldier (*Stratiotes aloides*), zones 6–9

Water violet (*Hottonia palustris*), zones 5–9

White snow-flake (*Nymphoides cristata*), zones 7–10

Yellow floating-heart (*Nymphoides peltata*), zones 7–10

Yellow snow-flake (*Nymphoides geminata*), zones 7–10

SUBMERGED PLANTS

Cabomba caroliniana, zones 6–10

Elodea canadensis, zones 5–10

Myriophyllum, zones 4–10

Saggitaria subulata, zones 5–10

Vallisneria americana, zones 4–10

20
Create a water garden with a pond

Water gardening has a venerable history, dating back approximately twenty-five hundred years to the Orient, where gardening first began, and spreading to ancient Egypt where the people cultivated lotus plants, papyrus, and water lilies. Water gardening was elevated to a high and expensive art form during the Renaissance in Europe, climaxing in the extravagant formal pools and fountains in the Tivoli Gardens in Rome and at Versailles in France.

A garden pond can be as small and simple or as large and elaborate as budget and space allow. Use it to cultivate water plants, or leave it empty and smooth to reflect the surrounding scene. Either way, a pond is an enchanting element in the garden.

In addition to being a beautiful focal point in your garden, a pond attracts all forms of intriguing wildlife, including birds and amphibians.

This heavily planted pond in a Japanese garden features Siberian iris and waterlilies. The mounding grass spilling over the water's edge is a beautiful textured transition between the wet and dry land.

Waterlilies are not the only flowers that can grace a garden pond. Here a large clump of the reed *Eriophorum* produces an abundance of white flowers in summer.

PROBLEM THREE:

Too Much Shade

Deep shade does not need to be a negative in your garden. On hot summer days, it provides a refreshing escape from direct sun and heat, and there is a wealth of plants, ranging from low-lying ground covers through annuals and perennials, shrubs, vines, and trees, that prefer shady conditions. In addition, there are steps you can take to bring more light into an area that is too dark.

Light and shade interact in different ways in the garden. It is possible to have an area in full shade (receiving no direct sun) that is actually quite bright because of reflected light. Such a location may actually support a wider variety of plants than a spot that gets an hour or two of direct sun but is very dark for the rest of the day. Shade is defined in several different ways. Dappled shade is a brightly lit environment where the sun makes its way through overhead foliage in random pools. A location that is shady for four to five hours a day is considered semi- or partly shaded. Full shade means little or no direct sun, but some reflected light, and dense shade is where the light is minimal.

Be aware of how many hours of sun, if any, your shady spot gets, and determine approximately how light or dark the shade is. Then choose plants accordingly. Remember, even among plants adapted to shade, some are more particular than others about how much light or shade they will tolerate.

21

Prune low branches to admit more light

Even shade-loving plants need light in order to grow. It is the intense midday sun they shrink from. By cutting off the lower branches of trees or bushes, you let in a surprising amount of beneficial light and allow the sun to strike the plants at the ideal times of day: early morning and late afternoon.

Create a shady planting area by pruning away the low branches of tall shrubs, and in a forested garden, create high shade by removing tree limbs up to as high as 40 feet, depending on the height of the trees. Underneath, you will have a protected area of dappled or bright shade that is ideal for many woodland shrubs and flowers. Thomas Jefferson took this approach, in fact, in the woodland section of his garden at Monticello. Writing to a friend, Jefferson described his ideas for adapting the open, naturalistic landscapes popularized by English landscape artists such as Capability Brown to the intense sun and heat of Virginia: "The only substitute I have been able to imagine is this. Let your ground be covered with trees of the loftiest stature. Trim up their bodies as high as the constitution & form of the tree will bear, but so as that their tops shall unite & yield dense shade. A wood, so open below, will have nearly the appearance of open grounds."

The lower branches of the trees in this small grove have been removed; thus the space is opened up and more light is admitted. Imagine what a tangle the space would be if the branches had been kept.

22

"Lace" trees to thin out branches and open up dense canopy

Rather than cut down a tree to bring in more light and air, "lace" the canopy by pruning away excess branches and twigs to remove the clutter. This procedure enhances the form of the tree, showing off its interesting structure, creating attractive tracery and at the same time allowing in more light.

Lacing a tree may seem a daunting task at first, but with a little thought and practice most people become adept at it. First, study the tree and decide which branches most enhance its shape and structure, and which ones may be removed. Begin working from the inside bottom, and work

The venerable Torrey pine trees in the background have been laced to allow light into this coastal San Diego shade garden. Fallen blossoms from a jacaranda tree carpet the lawn with lavender flowers.

A thirty-year-old twisted juniper has been thinned and shaped in a Japanese bonsai style to emphasize its fascinating structure and to allow light to reach the blooming impatiens planted at its feet.

your way up and out. Sometimes the decision about what to keep and what to remove is torturous. Alfredo Siani, who restored the two-hundred-year-old gardens of Oatlands Plantation near Leesburg, Virginia, admitted to deliberating a year or more over whether or not to remove some branches of ancient overgrown trees and shrubs. However, the rewards of lacing are many. A well-pruned tree will not only look better now, but will grow into a more graceful shape in the years to come.

23
Make use of shade-tolerant ground covers

There are alternatives to the reluctant lawn that has to be perpetually coaxed to grow in the shade. In addition to ivy, vinca, and pachysandra, consider crested iris (*Iris cristata*), a low-growing iris that covers the ground well and produces miniature flowers in spring; *Mazus reptans*, which blooms at the same time as crested iris; lily-of-the-valley (*Convallaria*); or baby's tears (*Soleirolia*).

In moist, deep shade where you are constantly battling moss, why not simply encourage it to grow and spread to develop a moss lawn? Moss is completely maintenance-free, requiring no mowing, fertilization, or irrigation. It will even withstand light foot traffic. To get it to spread, divide and plug the existing moss, or collect more from local woods and transplant it. Moss regenerates easily, so you need not worry about harming the woodland environment.

Pachysandra is a popular ground cover in shady areas, and for good reason. It requires little or no maintenance, and it makes a lush green cover too dense for weeds. It is one of the few plants that thrives under pines. There are also variegated cultivars with creamy white and green leaves.

Vinca is an easy-to-grow ground cover for shade, requires a minimum of water, and produces pretty blue flowers in spring.

24

Create a woodland garden of wildflowers and shrubs

Anyone fortunate enough to own a wooded property has a marvelous opportunity to create a garden using the delicate, charming plants found in the forest. The concept of woodland gardens evolved in the late nineteenth century, when English horticulturists

William Robinson and Gertrude Jekyll rebelled against the very formal styles popular in the Victorian era. They urged gardeners to plant natural gardens, especially on the fringes of their property to soften the transition between the cultivated garden and the untamed world outside.

In wild woods, plants tend to grow in a scramble, so that the delicate features of a special flower often are lost in the tangle. In a cultivated woodland garden, you can improve on nature by highlighting diminutive plants, positioning groupings, and showing off the enormous variety of plants available to their best advantage.

Top: Use azaleas and rhododendrons to give structure to a woodland garden. Note that the path has been covered with shredded bark, a material that looks at home in the setting and keeps down the weeds.

Above: Trillium and ferns are both superb choices for an eastern woodland garden. The azalea, which also thrives in wooded settings, is an excellent backdrop to the smaller plants in front.

You don't need a full forest on your property in order to enjoy a few woodland plants. Here, a clump of *Dicentra formosa*, a relative of Dutchman's breeches, makes a delicate display of soft pink blooms under a small tree in the spring.

25

Plant a foliage garden

In shade so deep that even shade-tolerant flowers won't bloom, plant a foliage garden that emphasizes the diversity of colors and textures available. "You have to have texture in a garden," advises W. F. Sinjen, a San Diego landscape designer. "When you have texture—greens and shades of green and texture of foliage—then you don't need so many flowers. If I were landscaping in the eastern United States, I'd use conifers to give gardens year-round texture."

To help brighten a dark corner, use variegated foliage, such as a green hosta with a creamy white edge on its leaves. The gold-spotted leaves of *Aucuba japonica* var. *variegata*, known as gold dust plant, look as if they're bathed in sunlight. They thrive in dark spots where little else will grow. For conifers that prefer shade, consider hemlock if they are not blight-afflicted in your region.

The heart-shaped leaves of the bishop's hat (*Epimedium*) contrast admirably with the feathery fronds of shield fern (*Polystichum*). Bishop's hat, which will spread to make an even, 9-inch-tall ground cover, flourishes in both dense shade and full sun. It is hardy to zone 3. The shield ferns, which are hardy to zone 4, are native to North American forests.

Hosta, Solomon's seal (*Polygonatum*), and maidenhair fern (*Adiantum pedatum*) combine beautifully in a shady foliage garden rich in color and texture. The maidenhair fern, which is hardy to zone 4, spreads by creeping root stalks, and makes an excellent choice for a ground cover in the shade.

26

Design an all-white or pastel garden to light up a shady corner

Perhaps the best-known white garden in the Western world was created in 1950 by Vita Sackville-West at her home in England, called Sissinghurst. There she planted fragrant roses, woolly lamb's ears, dusty millers, calla lilies, poppies, feverfew, and many other plants—all with white or gray blooms or foliage. While the white garden was being planted, she expressed some anxiety about its success, but now it is considered one of the most beautiful gardens in Great Britain.

White gardens are stunning at dusk, and also at night, when the flowers reflect the pale light of the moon. If you find it too hard to resist the pretty-colored flowers of some plant hybrids, then choose the lightest pastel shades to brighten a shady spot.

Add a touch of color in the shade with pastels such as the pink astilbe spires and lavender hydrangea blossoms growing in this woodland spot. The potted geranium on the table needs full sun, but it can take a few hours of shade while it serves as a centerpiece.

This combination of pink fuchsias and begonias is a cheerful splash of color in an otherwise dark spot. The flowers are all in pots because the dense network of roots of the pomegranate growing behind leaves no space in the soil for other plants.

There is something extra special about a garden of all-white flowers, especially when it brightens a dim, shady spot in the garden. Here, *Deutzia gracilis*, *Viburnum macrocephalum*, a white azalea, and tulip 'Maureen' bloom simultaneously with spectacular results.

27

Plant bulbs under deciduous trees

Many spring-blooming bulbs, including daffodils, grape hyacinths (*Muscari*), and snowflakes (*Leucojum*), require sun. However, they bloom early in the season before deciduous trees are fully in leaf, and their foliage has died back by the time the trees have created dense shade. These bulbs are ideal for a display of beautiful spring flowers in a place that otherwise would be too dark.

Winter aconite (*Eranthis hyemalis*) is an underused plant. In a setting that suits it, it will spread to create a blanket of golden flowers in early spring, sometimes even blooming through the snow. Plant winter aconite in drifts around trees, in rock gardens, or as a ground cover between stepping-stones.

These deciduous shrubs will create much too dense a cover for flowers when they are in leaf, but the early-blooming purple crocus, followed in a few weeks by daffodils, have plenty of room and light to flourish through their cycle before the leaves of the shrubs intrude.

Shade-tolerant plants

TREES AND SHRUBS

Azalea, zones 5–9

Camellia, zones 7–10

Canadian hemlock (*Tsuga canadensis*), zones 4–8

Euonymus fortunei, zones 5–9

Ficus, zones 9–10

Flowering dogwood (*Cornus florida*), zones 5–8

Gardenia jasminoides, zones 8–10

Holly (*Ilex*), hardiness varies

Hydrangea, zones 6–10

Leucothoe, zones 5–9

Mahonia, zones 5–10

Mountain laurel (*Kalmia latifolia*), zones 5–9

Osmanthus, zones 6–9

Pieris, zones 6–9

Redbud (*Cercis canadensis*), zones 5–9

Rhododendron, zones 5–9

Sweetbay magnolia (*Magnolia virginiana*), zones 6–9

Viburnum species, zones 4–9

Yew (*Taxus*), zones 5–7

ANNUALS, BULBS, AND PERENNIALS

Ajuga, zones 3–8

Anemone hybrids, zones 6–9

Angelica (*Angelica archangelica*), zones 4–8

Arum, zones 7–9

Astilbe, zones 5–8

Bellflower (*Campanula*), zones 4–8

Begonia, annual

Bergenia, zones 3–8

Bleeding-heart (*Dicentra*), zones 4–8

Bloodroot (*Sanguinaria canadensis*), zones 3–9

British Columbia wild ginger (*Asarum caudatum*), zones 6–8

Caladium bicolor, zone 10 or as annual

Coleus hybridus, zone 10 or as annual

Cyclamen hederifolium, zones 5–9

Epimedium, zones 5–9

Ferns, hardiness varies

Fuchsia, zones 9–10 or as annual

Hosta, zones 4–9

Impatiens wallerana, annual

Lady's-mantle (*Alchemilla vulgaris*), zones 3–7

Leopard plant (*Ligularia tussilaginea* 'Aureomaculata'), zones 4–8

Lily-of-the-valley (*Convallaria majalis*), zones 4–9

Lilyturf (*Liriope*), zones 5–10

Loosestrife (*Lysimachia nummularia* 'Aurea'), zones 4–8

Lungwort (*Pulmonaria*), zones 5–8

Mondo grass (*Ophiopogon japonicus*), zones 7–10

Pachysandra terminalis, zones 5–8

Periwinkle (*Vinca minor*), zones 4–8

Phlox divaricata, zones 4–8

Primrose rose (*Rosa primula*), zones 5–7

Scilla bifolia, zones 3–8

Terrestrial orchid (*Bletilla striata*), zones 5–8

Violet (*Viola*), zones 4–8

28

Create a garden for a dry-shade area

Dry shade is typically caused by trees that take the moisture from the ground, at the same time blocking the sun with their foliage. The problem can be ameliorated by adding organic material to the soil, particularly cow or horse manure, to improve moisture retention.

Many plants grow in dry shade. For color, try impatiens, although it will wilt if it gets too dry. Vinca is another good choice and produces pretty periwinkle-blue flowers in spring. In warm climates, clivia, which blooms best when rootbound, produces vibrant orange flowers. Some of the excellent foliage plants for dry shade include ivy, bergenia (which produces its best leaf color in poor soil), and coleus.

With dappled sun, drought-tolerant flowers such as this medley of pink-blooming red valerian (*Centranthus ruber*) and pincushion flower (*Scabiosa*) growing under a small bottlebrush tree will bloom beautifully.

29

Create a garden for a moist-shade area

Many plants are well adapted to grow and bloom in moist shade. Among the shrubs that like damp ground are Carolina allspice (*Calycanthus*) and sweet pepperbush (*Clethra alnifolia*), both with deliciously fragrant flowers. Hollies and mahonia will also tolerate wet soil.

For perennials and annuals, look to astilbe, Virginia bluebells (*Mertensia*), lobelia, Japanese iris (*Iris kaempferi*), marsh marigold (*Caltha palustris*), and mimulus.

Hostas, ferns, and *Phlox divaricata* grow well in this moist, shady spot.

30

Use light-colored paving or walls to reflect light into shaded areas

Light is a critical factor in plant growth. By increasing the light by as little as 1 percent, you can improve the growth and flowering of your plants by as much as 100 percent. One way to get more light into a dark corner is to use white or light-colored paving. Not only does the paving brighten up the space visually, it also reflects whatever light is present, increasing its intensity and benefiting the growth of sturdier and healthier plants.

By the same token, a dark wall not only deepens the sense of gloom pervading an area already in dense shade, it may cause a sunless environment if it is blocking the light. Ameliorate the problem by painting the wall a light color, such as white or a pale pastel.

This garden, which is surrounded by high trees as well as the wall, would feel dark and oppressive were it not for the wall's bright white surface.

31

Hang shade-loving plants in baskets to lift the color area

Hanging baskets spilling over with bloom can transform a space. The city of Victoria, British Columbia, has made a name for itself in part because of the flowering baskets that hang from each lamppost along the harbor. Lots of color at eye level or a little above, is a wonderfully appealing feature in a garden—or almost anywhere.

Fill baskets or pots with shade-tolerant flowers such as fuchsias, begonias, impatiens, forget-me-nots, ageratum, and nicotiana, and hang them from tree branches, where they can enjoy the dappled light filtering through the leaves. These baskets may also adorn a covered patio or the walls on the north side of a house.

The light filtering through this trellis is ideal for these hanging fuchsias, which bring color up to eye level and break the monotony of the bare trellis.

PROBLEM FOUR:

Ongoing Pest Damage

The war against insect pests is never-ending, and the insects often appear to be on the winning side. It's impossible and undesirable to completely eradicate insects from the garden, but you can take preventive measures to keep them at a minimum. A poorly maintained garden is a haven for insects that nest and lay eggs in dead plant material and discarded prunings. Keep the garden clean; remove all plant debris. Plants that are healthy are more resilient when damaged by pests, and some varieties of plants are actually resistant to or tolerant of specific pests and diseases. In any case, inspect your plants regularly for signs of pests and disease, and keep infested plants out of the garden. It's easier to control just the vanguard scouts than a full-blown invasion.

In the case of the larger mammalian pests, most gardeners are torn between the sentimental appeal of furry creatures and their resentment of the plant-destroying wildlife. The challenging goal is to find ways to encourage these animals to live their lives safely away from your garden.

32

Use plants deer avoid

The deer motto may well be "Desperate times call for desperate measures." When food is scarce, they will eat almost any plant, even those that make them sick. Nevertheless, there are some plants that deer are less likely to devour, and they are your safest bets in gardens where marauding deer are a problem.

Deer tend to avoid certain bulbs, including leucojum, iris, daffodils and narcissus, and calla lilies. Many sources also include tulips as a bulb deer despise. The browsing animals ignore the foliage, but eat the flowers with relish, leaving the topped stems. Other flowers deer tend to avoid are agapanthus, calendula, foxglove, lupines, some poppy varieties, California fuchsias (*Zauschneria*), pride of Madeira (*Echium*), hellebores, and zinnias.

The plants deer generally find unpalatable include ferns, boxwood, buddleia (*Buddleia davidii*), Carolina allspice (*Calycanthus floridus*), Mexican orange

These lupines mix well with other flowers deer dislike, including iris and foxgloves.

The aloes, succulent members of the lily family, are another plant group that deer consider unpalatable.

(*Choisya*), rock rose (*Cistus*) shrubs and vines from the jasmine family, rosemary, junipers, kerria, oleander (*Nerium*), mahonia, and lantana. Curiously, deer avoid rhododendrons but savor their close relative, azaleas. They generally won't eat the spiky fronds of Mediterranean fan palm. Among vining plants that are considered safe from deer are Carolina jessamine (*Gelsemium*), English ivy, potato vine (*Solanum jasminoides*), Costa Rican nightshade (*Solanum wendlandii*), and cape honeysuckle (*Tecomaria capensis*).

Daffodils, such as this clump of *Narcissus cyclamineus* 'Jack Snipe', are a good choice for deer-safe flowers in spring.

This attractive grouping of iris and foxgloves should be deer-proof, except when other food is very scarce.

33

Use deterrents for deer, mice, moles, voles, and rabbits

Fencing can keep deer, mice, and rabbits out of a garden. Since deer can jump high vertically, but not horizontally, you will need to build a fence at least 8 feet high or create a barrier 5 feet high and wide to keep them out of the garden. Rabbits can be kept out with wire mesh no larger than 1½ inches, although in addition to the 2 feet above the ground,

the wire should be buried at least 6 inches under the soil. Mice require a mesh no larger than ¼ inch, and the barrier should extend 1 foot above and below the soil. (To keep mice from eating your bulbs, toss a handful of gravel into each planting hole with the bulb. The sharp edges will hurt their noses.)

If an 8-foot fence is not to your liking to keep out deer, you might try running rope in crisscross patterns from tree to tree during the winter months when food is scarce, to confuse them. Protect tender saplings by surrounding them with wire mesh.

The best way to keep moles and voles out of your garden is to reduce their food supply by controlling insect grubs in the soil under your lawn.

34

Set traps in the garden

If a specific animal is creating undue problems, or if passive control is not working, you may want to resort to traps in your garden. You can choose from a vast array of traps specifically designed to catch different kinds of animals. Live traps, which capture the animal without injuring it and allow you to merely move the intruder from your area to another, appeal to many people. In other cases, such as instances of sickness or injury, it may be preferable to have the animal in question destroyed. Your local state or county cooperative extension service should have information on the types of traps available and the regulations concerning the control of the wildlife pests in your area.

The netting stretched over these raised vegetable beds should be adequate to keep out rabbits, deer, and hungry birds.

35

Surround your garden with diatomaceous earth or wood ashes

Diatomaceous earth, a mineral created from the remains of fossilized diatoms, is an effective medium for controlling caterpillars, slugs, snails, borers, leafhoppers, and thrips. Its sharp edges puncture the soft bodies of these creatures, causing them to die from dehydration. Diatomaceous earth is completely harmless to people, other animals, and birds. Spread the material on the ground as a barrier around the plants or garden beds. Use only horticultural grade diatomaceous earth, not the kind that's been treated for swimming-pool filters.

Wood ashes also have sharp edges that kill soft-bodied creatures. Check the soil's pH before using wood ashes. If applied in large quantities, they will increase the soil's alkalinity.

Plants to attract birds

TREES

Acacia, zones 8–10

Albizia, zones 9–10

Alder (*Alnus*), zones 4–7

Allegheny serviceberry (*Amelanchier laevis*), zones 5–7

American hornbeam (*Carpinus caroliniana*), zones 3–9

Arbutus, zones 7–9

Ash (*Sorbus*), zones 3–8

Birch (*Betula*), zones 3–8

California pepper (*Schinus molle*), zones 9–10

Cherry (*Prunus*), zones 3–9

Chinaberry (*Melia azedarach*), zones 7–10

Crab apple (*Malus*) zones 4–8

Dogwood (*Cornus*), zones 2–8

Elder (*Sambucus*), zones 4–9

Elm (*Ulmus*), zones 3–9

European beech (*Fagus sylvatica*), zones 4–7

Fir (*Abies*), zones 4–8

Hackberry (*Celtis*), zones 2–9

Hawthorn (*Crataegus*), zones 4–8

Larch (*Larix*), zones 3–6

Loquat (*Eriobotrya japonica*), zones 8–10

Mulberry (*Morus*), zones 5–9

Oak (*Quercus*), zones 6–10

Pine (*Pinus*), zones 4–10

Spruce (*Picea*), zones 3–8

SHRUBS

Abutilon, zones 7–10

Bird-of-paradise shrub (*Caesalpinia gillesii*), zone 10

Bottlebrush (*Callistemon citrinus*), zones 9–10

Blueberry (*Vaccinium*), zones 2–9

Buddleia, zones 5–9

Callicarpa, zones 6–8

Ceanothus, zones 7–10

Cotoneaster species, zones 5–9

Currant (*Ribes*), zones 5–9

Elaeagnus, zones 2–9

Euonymus, zones 4–10

Firethorn (*Pyracantha*), zones 6–9

Flowering raspberry (*Rubus deliciosus*), zones 5–8

Flowering quince (*Chaenomeles*), zone 10

Garrya, zones 8–10

Gaultheria, zones 6–8

Grevillea lanigera, zone 10

Holly (*Ilex*), hardiness varies

Manzanita (*Arctostaphylos*), zones 2–8

Natal plum (*Carissa grandiflora*), zones 9–10

Ocean-spray (*Holodiscus discolor*), zones 6–9

Photinia, zones 5–10

Pineapple guava (*Feijoa sellowiana*), zones 9–10

Privet (*Ligustrum*), zones 5–10

Red chokeberry (*Aronia arbutifolia*), zones 4–8

Toyon (*Heteromeles arbutifolia*), zones 8–10

Viburnum, zones 3–9

36

Create a garden to attract insect-eating birds

Insect-eating birds, especially when they are hunting for their young as well as for themselves, are one of the best natural means of keeping insect pests under control in the garden. Among the familiar birds that enjoy an insect diet are catbirds, mockingbirds, cardinals, and brown thrashers. The best way to attract these birds to your garden is to provide comfortable nesting spots for them, cover from predators, and water.

Plant densely branched shrubs, such as forsythia, mock orange, evergreens, box honeysuckle, privet, and lilacs, where the birds can safely nest and hide. For an added bonus, select from among the many plants, such as pyracantha and barberry, that also provide berries to vary the avian diet and provide food in winter when insects are scarce.

This tight grouping of shrubs and perennials is attractive to birds looking for protective cover and safe nesting.

Insect-eating birds also enjoy fruit and berries for variety. A fruiting tree, such as this crabapple, is a popular dining spot for many birds.

PROBLEM FIVE:

Soil Limitations

Poor soil, either too high in clay content or too sandy, too alkaline or too acid, is an almost universal challenge facing gardeners. It's the source of the old adage that states, "Put a five-dollar plant into a ten-dollar hole." This is good advice; if you have invested money in a plant, it is wise to invest even more in creating an environment where it can thrive. That's why successful gardeners, even those with good-quality soil, never put a spade into the ground without adding some manure or other organic material.

Initially most garden plots need a major addition of compost, manure, and other organic material to transform the soil into the crumbly loam that is ideal for growing plants. The rule of thumb for major soil amendment is to add a volume of amendment equal to 25 to 50 percent of the soil volume to be cultivated.

Do the first digging of a new garden by hand rather than with a garden tiller. Most of the machines sold for homeowners cannot dig deeply enough when the earth is still firm. Hand digging is exhausting, but it has its benefits, both physical and mental. As the French author Colette wrote in her novel *Break of Day*, "To lift and penetrate and tear apart the soil is a labor—a pleasure—always accompanied by an exaltation that no unprofitable exercise can ever provide....The earth you open up has no longer any past—only a future."

37

In acid soil, grow plants that like a low pH

Soil with a low pH, called acid, is generally found in regions of heavy rainfall. Typically, the soil is either sandy, or in a wooded area where it contains large amounts of organic matter. Most plants will tolerate mildly acidic soil; however, if soil tests indicate a very low pH, you may want to mix in some lime to bring the balance closer to neutral. Once you've added lime, you need to be careful to use fertilizers that do not have an acid reaction.

The other option is to grow plants that thrive in acid soil. While gardeners with alkaline soil are pouring on acid-type fertilizers and chelates to keep azaleas, rhododendrons, and camellias thriving, yours will do very nicely on their own. See the following list of other plants that thrive in acid soil.

Brunnera, with its airy clusters of tiny clear-blue spring flowers, and heather are two good choices when the soil pH is low.

Cassiope, a member of the heather family, is an ideal candidate for a shaded spot in a rock garden with acid soil.

The evergreen lithodora makes a wonderful ground cover in acid soil, especially in May and June, when it flowers in brilliant blue.

Plants for neutral to acid soil

TREES

Chilean fire brush (*Embothrium coccineum*), zones 9–10

Douglas fir (*Pseudotsuga menziesii*), zones 5–7

Fir (*Abies*), zones 4–8

Golden larch (*Pseudolarix amabilis*), zones 5–9

Japanese snowbell (*Styrax japonica*), zones 5–9

Madroña (*Arbutus menziesii*), zones 7–9

Pine (*Pinus*), zones 4–10

Spruce (*Picea*), zones 3–8

Stewartia, zones 6–9

Western hemlock (*Tsuga heterophylla*), zones 6–8

SHRUBS

Azalea, zones 5–9

Blueberry (*Vaccinium*), zones 2–9

Camellia, zones 7–10

Desfontainea spinosa, zones 9–10

Epacris impressa, zones 8–9

Gaultheria, zones 6–8

Leucothöe, zones 5–9

Pernettya, zones 7–9

Philesia magellanica, zones 7–8

Pieris, zones 6–9

Rhododendron, zones 5–9

Styrax, zones 7–10

Waratah (*Telopea speciosissima*), zone 10

Zenobia pulverulenta, zones 6–9

ROCK PLANTS

Alpine azalea (*Loiseleuria procumbens*), zones 2–5

Androsace vandellii, zones 4–7

Bearberry (*Arctostaphylos uva-ursi*), zones 2–8

Bird's-foot violet (*Viola pedata*), zones 3–8

Bog rosemary (*Andromeda polifolia*), zones 2–6

Celmisia, zones 9–10

Corydalis cashmeriana, zones 6–8

Dwarf arctic birch (*Betula nana*), zones 2–5

Epigaea, zones 3–9

Galax urceolata, zones 5–8

Gaultheria, zones 4–7

Gentiana sino-ornata, zones 5–7

Cassiope, zones 2–7

Lewisia, zones 6–7

Lingonberry (*Vaccinium vitis-idaea*), zones 2–5

Lithodora diffusa, zones 6–8

Maianthemum canadense, zones 4–8

Ourisia, zones 7–8

Pernettya, zones 7–9

Phlox adsurgens, zones 4–8

Phyllodoce, zones 2–8

Rhodothamnus chamaecistus, zone 7

Rock pink (*Dianthus pavonius*), zones 4–6

Shortia, zones 5–9

Twinflower (*Linnaea borealis*), zones 3–6

38

In alkaline soil, grow plants that tolerate a high pH

Soil is considered alkaline if the pH ranges between 7.5 and 8.5. An even higher pH, up to 9.0 (the highest pH at which plants can grow) is considered alkali or strongly alkaline. Such soil is high in calcium carbonate (lime) and other minerals such as sodium. Alkaline conditions are generally found in areas of light rainfall—the less rainfall, the higher the pH. Some plants will grow where the pH is extremely high, but your best bet is to plant in raised beds and containers filled with good topsoil.

The choice of plants that grow in moderate to low alkalinity is wider, and if the pH is closer to neutral, you can even grow acid-soil plants by using acid-type fertilizers and chelates, as well as adding peat moss, ground bark, or sawdust to the soil. See the plant list for suggestions.

Lupines, whether planted *en masse* or as specimens in a perennial bed, are a fabulous addition to a garden with alkaline soil.

Fountain grass (*Pennisetum*) is growing in popularity as a landscape plant as people learn to appreciate its many merits, not the least of which is its adaptability to alkaline soil.

Alkaline soil is often found in areas of little rainfall. Drought-tolerant plants such as this 'Alan Chickering' sage do well. Other possibilities are oleander, olive, pomegranate, loquat, bottlebrush, and blue palo verde.

56

39

Grow plants that tolerate clay soil

Clay soil is appropriately referred to as heavy soil because it is a very dense combination of microscopic mineral particles. There is little space between the fine particles, so wet clay soils drain and dry out slowly. A benefit of clay is that the soil is high in mineral nutrients that aren't leached out by rapid draining. On the negative side, plant roots have to work hard to push through the heavy material, and they don't get much oxygen.

You can improve clay by adding sand and other coarse organic materials to loosen and lighten the soil, and to improve drainage and the availability of oxygen. Also, some plants are well adapted to this heavy growing medium. See the plant list for some possibilities.

Mahonia comes in a wide range of types, some adapted to cold climates, others preferring the desert. Each has its own attractive features, and all do well in heavy soil.

Whether planted alone as a fascinating specimen or massed in a tight row to provide a screen, as shown here, the Atlas cedar (*Cedrus atlantica* 'Glauca Pendula') is a good choice for heavy soil.

Plants for poor soil

ALKALINE SOIL
(A pH rating from 7.5 to 8.5.) Plants marked with an asterisk (*) also take heavy clay soil.

Bottlebrush (*Callistemon*), zones 8–10

Cape plumbago (*Plumbago capensis*), zones 9–10

Creeping coprosma (*Coprosma kirkii*), zones 8–10

*Cypress (*Cupresses* species), zones 7–10

*English lavender (*Lavandula angustifolia*), zones 6–9

Fountain grass (*Pennisetum* species), zones 5–10

*Juniper (*Juniperus* species), zones 3–10

Lantana, zones 9–10

Loquat (*Eriobotrya* species), zones 8–10

Oleander (*Nerium oleander*), zones 8–10

*Oregon grape (*Mahonia aquifolium*), zones 6–9

Rock rose (*Cistus* varieties), zones 7–9

*St. John's-wort (*Hypericum* species), zones 6–9

Sweet alyssum (*Lobularia maritima*), annual

Sweet bay (*Laurus nobilis*), zones 8–10

HEAVY CLAY SOILS

Atlas cedar (*Cedrus atlantica*), zones 7–9

Ceanothus, zones 8–10

Chinese photinia (*Photinia serratifolia*), zones 7–9

Cotoneaster species, zones 5–9

Crape myrtle (*Lagerstroemia indica*), zones 7–10

Firethorn (*Pyracantha* species), zones 6–10

Leyland cypress (**x** *Cupressocyparis leylandii*), zones 6–9

Monkey flower (*Mimulus* species), zones 6–10

Oak (*Quercus* species), zones 5–10

Tree mallow (*Lavatera assurgentiflora*), zones 9–10

SANDY SOIL

Wormwood (*Artemisia ludoviciana*), zones 5–8

Barberry (*Berberis empetrifolia*), zones 7–9

Bird-of-paradise flower (*Strelitzia reginae*), zones 9–10

Catmint (*Nepeta* **x** *faassenii*), zones 4–8

Chinaberry (*Melia azedarach*), zones 7–10

Rock rose (*Cistus*), zones 7–9

Great globe thistle (*Echinops sphaerocephalus*), zones 3–9

Judas tree (*Cercis siliquastrum*), zones 8–9

Sea lavender (*Limonium latifolium* 'Blue Cloud'), zones 4–9

Marigold (*Tagetes*), annual

Oriental poppy (*Papaver orientale*), zones 4–9

Portulaca grandiflora, annual

Red valerian (*Centranthus ruber*), zones 5–9

Silver wattle (*Acacia dealbata*), zones 9–10

Spiny bear's breech (*Acanthus spinosus*), zones 5–9

40

Grow plants that tolerate sandy soil

Sandy soil is comprised of large, rounded particles. As a result, the structure is loose, and the soil drains well and warms up easily. However, sandy soil requires frequent watering, which leaches out valuable nutrients. Organic amendments, such as compost and manure, help sandy soils to retain water and nutrients, as well as add to fertility.

Typically found very near the coast and in desert regions, a host of plants are well adapted to this growing medium. Cacti and succulents, which are able to go for long periods without water, do very well in quick-draining sand. Among the annuals, perennials, and biennials try coreopsis, cleome, impatiens, Shirley poppies, dianthus, verbena, marigolds, and lavender.

Pride of Madeira (*Echium*), which blooms in May and June, is an excellent plant for warm-climate seacoast gardens where the soil is sandy.

41

If your soil is rocky, plant among the rocks

Instead of fighting a rocky terrain by trying to remove all the stones, turn them into an asset by creating a rock garden. Also called *rockeries*, rock gardens are an ideal way to showcase small, shallow-rooted plants. Choose the minor bulbs (the smaller tulips, daffodils, and iris), crocus, anemone, glory-of-the-snow (*Chionodoxa*), and snowdrops (*Galanthus*). Other good rock garden plants include heathers, small woodland flowers, low-growing sedums, and saxifrage. Consider planting dwarf conifers as well to give height and scale to the design.

A dry stone wall offers another opportunity for a rock garden. Use a chopstick or other narrow tool to carefully push the plant roots into the crevices between stones. Yellow alyssum, also called basket-of-gold (*Aurinia saxatilis*), and *Phlox subulata* are both good choices because they will cascade down the sides of the wall, covering it with bloom in the spring.

Instead of undertaking the back-breaking task of removing the rocks on this hillside, the home-owner wisely opted to create an attractive rock garden.

These blooming clumps of *Aubri-eta deltoidea*, basket-of-gold (*Aurinia saxatilis*), *Phlox subulata*, *Sedum spathulifolium*, and dwarf wallflowers (*Cheiranthus*) make a dazzling spring display in this rock garden.

42

Create your own soil amendment by adding compost

Composting was first introduced two thousand years ago by Marcus Cato, a Roman statesman who wanted to build soil fertility throughout the Roman Empire. You can improve the fertility of your own garden plot with composting, using nature's own process of decomposition to transform "garden waste" into garden gold.

Not only is composting a sound horticultural practice, creating a rich soil amendment from recycled garden trimmings, pulled weeds, and fallen leaves, but it is also environmentally sound, reducing pressure on landfills, where garden waste represents a huge percentage of the bulk.

There are approximately 130 composting bins currently on the market, ranging from small systems suitable for pocket-sized gardens (even on rooftops) to large, triple-compartment bins that divide fresh, processed, and mature processed compost. Choose the one that suits you best, or go the more simple route by piling up garden trimmings and kitchen scraps (don't overlook egg shells and coffee grounds, but avoid fats and meat products). To successfully decompose, the material needs air, moisture, and bacteria. Fluff up the pile periodically, turning over chunks with a pitchfork to let in air. Leave the top slightly convex to collect rainwater, or sprinkle the pile with a hose periodically to keep the material moist. A balanced recipe of nitrogen-rich materials (dry leaves, straw, and dry grass clippings) will get the inherent bacteria working faster, but if getting the right mix is too complicated for you, you can invest in a commercial innoculant that will help speed up the process, regardless of the content of your pile.

Because of its many uses, it's virtually impossible to have too much compost. It makes an excellent mulch, soil amendment, and top dressing for lawns (spread it ¼ inch thick in lieu of fertilizer).

43

Plant in raised beds

Hardpan, *claypan*, and *caliche* are all terms for a nearly impenetrable layer of soil. In gardens where this layer is very near the surface, the best option is to create raised beds. A raised bed may be a simple mound of topsoil, contained by stones around the perimeter, or an elaborate, deep planter made of stone, brick, cement, or wood. The depth of your raised bed should be

governed by what you want to plant. Small trees require from 1½ to 3 feet of soil; most annuals can get by with as little as 6 to 8 inches. If the raised bed has a solid enclosure, be sure to install adequate drainage so the plants won't drown.

This collection of raised flower beds was designed in the tradition of American Colonial gardens, laid out in symmetrical quadrants.

In the Southwest, the common natural layer of impervious soil is called *caliche*. This gardener solved the problem with an attractive raised bed that marries well with the architecture of the home.

PROBLEM SIX:

Lack of Space

As land grows scarcer and more expensive, home lots are getting smaller. Suburban dwellers, as well as city denizens, are facing the challenge of creating gardens in pocket-handkerchief-sized spaces. Some homeowners find it a relief to have less land to maintain; others chafe at the discipline of exercising their gardening urges in such a limited space.

But frustrated gardeners can take heart. An extraordinary number and variety of plants can fit into a small area, and a lush, profusely blooming look is much more economical to achieve in limited quarters. You also can make what space you do have look larger with the clever use of illusions and a sensitivity to scale.

"Illusion is everything in a garden," says W. F. Sinjen, a landscape designer in San Diego, California, who has transformed his own 40-by-100-foot lot into a tropical forest full of winding paths that loop back on themselves to increase the sense of space. To maintain proportion, he shortened his garden chair legs by 4 inches, "to bring them down to Mother Earth, and to fit the scale of the garden."

44

Fool the eye by planting dwarf shrubs and conifers to make space appear larger

Dwarf shrubs and conifers are marvelous in a tiny garden because they have all the beautiful qualities of form and texture of their larger counterparts but are in correct scale for the smaller space.

Dwarf conifers are a particularly rich and diverse group of plants. Colors range from blues and grays through the wide spectrum of greens to beautiful golden yellows. There is a form for almost any need: conical, prostrate and spreading, mounding, drooping, and pyramiding upright. Texture, an important element that is often overlooked in gardens, is another of their varied assets. Look for spikes, feathers, fans, delicate detail, and broad strong strokes.

In addition to their aesthetic attributes, dwarf conifers require very little maintenance and provide year-round interest. Plant them as features in their own right, or in a rock garden to provide scale and to act as a foil for bulbs and other small-sized plants.

This grouping of small conifers planted with heather illustrates just some of the choices of color, form, and texture available in the dwarf conifer world.

45

Stagger plant heights for an illusion of greater depth

Staggering plant heights not only gives the illusion of greater depth but also allows you to have a wider selection of plants in a small space. Start at the back with a vine, a tall shrub, or a small tree. If you use a shrub, choose one that won't spread so much that it will intrude on the rest of the space. In front of it, plant something shorter, and continue layering in this manner, finishing off with low-growing shrubs or edging plants such as sweet alyssum or dianthus. If you run out of ground before you run out of plants, place the overflow in pots at the front of your beds.

Opposite: This narrow woodland planting of short phlox in front backed by the taller growing weigela, *Viburnum plicatum*, and yew provides an effective buffer from the house next door.

Below: The many plants squeezed into this tiny perennial border all show off to good advantage because of their staggered heights. Clematis 'Jackmanii' climbs the trellis in back and alstroemeria, campanula, lady's mantle (*Alchemilla*), and geranium are planted according to height in front.

46

Create an illusion of greater depth by planting warm colors up front and cool colors in back

Make color theory work for you to create an illusion of space. Generally speaking, warm colors seem to advance, appearing closer than they really are, and cool colors seem to recede. So put bright red, yellow, orange, pink, or gold flowers in the front of a small garden, and put flowers and foliage with the softer shades of blue and lavender toward the back. The cool colors will retreat into the background, fooling the eye into perceiving more space.

The climbing *Hydrangea anomala* subsp. *petiolaris* covers this otherwise stark wall. This attractive vine provides the middle layer of this terraced space-saving planting of rhododendrons on top and viburnum down below.

The cool blue of the spruce tree appears to recede, so that the tree seems more distant than it really is, especially in contrast to the warm yellow of the potentilla in front.

47

Create optical illusions with paving to give a greater sense of depth

The understanding of perspective revolutionized painting in the Renaissance. Among the techniques the artists mastered was causing objects painted or drawn on flat surfaces to look farther away by making them smaller than objects positioned in the foreground of the pictorial space. That same principle can be employed with plants and architectural elements to dramatically increase the sense of space in a small garden.

Smaller paving stones or bricks will look farther away; larger ones will appear closer. Use a combination of sizes, placing the smallest stones at the farthest end of the garden, to visually lengthen the distance and give a greater feeling of open space to patio and garden areas surrounding your home.

It is only 12 feet from the house to the back wall, but because the bricks are cut shorter near the wall and gradually increase in length to normal as they approach the house, when viewed from the house, this patio appears deeper than it really is.

48

Create paths that loop back on themselves

Even in a very small space, it is possible to have a "stroll garden" that leads from one magical spot to another. The secret is to have the paths loop back upon themselves, with dense plantings in the small space between the two sections of path to disguise the fact that they are so close. Choose the longest distance between two points, allowing your trail to meander.

Along the way, place a statuette, a bird bath, or an exotic plant to draw the eye and to make you want to reach that place. Choose another special spot, and allow the path to spread into a small, plant-enclosed patio. This sequestered retreat may become a favorite place to sit in your garden.

In addition to making your garden feel bigger, paths that curve out of sight, beckoning the stroller to follow, add the important element of mystery to a garden.

Place an interesting object, such as this charming birdhouse, to create a focal point along a garden path.

66

49

Use all available planting space, even awkward long and narrow beds

The narrow strip of land left beside a paved driveway and the 10-foot-wide passage along the side of your house that separates your property from your neighbor's are both awkward spaces that tend to be neglected in home gardens.

However, when space is at a premium, these spots provide important opportunities for pretty landscaping. They are also built-in illusions waiting for development since their narrowness tends to make them appear longer than they actually are. If you want to maintain that illusion of stretching a long way, don't break up the space. On page 22, the photograph at bottom left shows the dry stone river bed as an uninterrupted element running down a narrow space, making it feel longer, especially as it curves out of sight at the far end.

The pruned lower trunks of this bougainvillea, which have been trained to grow on a two-dimensional plane, make a striking silhouette against this bare wall, while the dense top makes a floral screen from the neighbors. The ground cover running the length of the space unifies it and softens the hard edges of the long wall and paving.

50

Save space by planting vegetables, herbs, and flowers together

Unlike oil and water, flowers and vegetables do mix—with great success. In fact, many vegetables, such as red-stemmed Swiss chard, artichokes, and scarlet runner beans, are attractive in their own right. Equally, some herbs, such as sage and chives, produce flowers worthy of an ornamental border, and curly parsley has an exceptionally pretty leaf.

Plant French marigolds among the vegetables to repel nematodes, the microscopic soil worm that attacks the roots of plants, and include a crimson-red flower, such as a snapdragon, in the vegetable garden to highlight the deep red stalks of 'Ruby' Swiss chard.

In addition, let the edible plants do double duty as ornamentals. Edible strawberries

Leeks, garlic, summer squash, lettuce, zinnias, and cosmos make a happy combination of flowers and vegetables.

make a fine ground cover. Try the recently introduced 'Pink Panda', which produces pink flowers throughout the summer, or *fraises des bois*. Creeping thyme is an edible ground cover that will take some foot traffic. Attractive fruit-bearing trees are a good choice for landscaping. Save space with dwarf fruit trees, and if space is really at a premium, espalier them against a fence or wall. Serious gardeners can extend the fruiting season with trees grafted with branches of different varieties, such as an early- and late-producing apple on the same tree.

The glaucous green of the ruffled black-seeded Simpson lettuce is a beautiful foliage accent in this garden of blooming violas, daisies, candytuft (*Iberis*), and toadflax (*Linaria*).

51

Augment space by growing some plants in pots

You can buy yourself more gardening space, and achieve some very nice special effects, with the effective use of a wide variety of containers and potted plants.

Be creative in what you choose to hold the plants. Tillandsias, which don't need soil, will live happily attached to the bowls of wooden spoons. Hang them above the kitchen sink, where they will get the moisture from steam. Large shells, such as clam and conch, can host shallow-rooted plants. Put flowers in a picturesque old wheelbarrow or a watering can with a rusted-out bottom. A hollowed-out log makes an attractive, rustic container, as does an old wicker basket. The possibilities are limitless.

These bountiful pots of blooms are a colorful addition to this small entry. Changed easily with the seasons, they always look their best.

52

Plant an all-container garden on a deck, patio, porch, or rooftop

Having no ground in which to plant needn't stop anyone from having a garden. An amazing number of plants can be grown in containers. Don't limit yourself to traditional flowers. Small trees and shrubs, vines, vegetables, and herbs all do well in pots.

In the vegetable kingdom, new hybrids are being introduced that are especially designed and developed for small-space gardens and containers. 'Tom Thumb' lettuce is a compact head lettuce, and 'Ruby' and 'Salad Bowl', with their frilly leaves, do well in hanging baskets and window boxes. 'Pixie' tomatoes have medium-sized fruit and short, compact vines ideal for containers. Even deep-rooted vegetables such as carrots, which

Bring life to the stark emptiness of a deck, balcony, or patio with clusters of pots filled with blooming flowers.

traditionally have not been recommended for pots, have been hybridized so that shorter varieties are now available to grow in soil as shallow as 8 inches. Look for the variety called 'Short 'n Sweet'. Watermelon has been scaled down so that you can now grow one 'Sugar Bush' plant in a 15-gallon tub and expect to get three substantial, juicy melons. Nowadays, it isn't hard to have a moveable feast straight from the garden.

A window box is a marvelous way to create planting space where there is none, and to bring a floral view to the window. Cram window boxes full to make them look bountiful, and then water with diluted fertilizer to give the extra boost of nutrients the crowded plants need.

PROBLEM SEVEN:

Too Much Space

Too much space can be just as troublesome as too little. In most cases, a garden wants to be of human scale, with intimate spots and retreats. Wide-open vistas that stretch as far as the eye can see are appealing, but people also need smaller areas where the scene can be absorbed in a glance.

A large garden offers the opportunity to meet both needs. Open spaces and long vistas created by *allées* can be combined with intimate garden rooms and secluded seating areas. Gardeners with lots of land can create gardens with different moods and themes: a casual cottage garden and one with geometric, formal lines; a shade garden and a water garden; a garden that features a special plant collection and a rockery that highlights tiny flowers. To keep from getting overwhelmed, both by the number of possibilities and the effort required, develop the garden a little at a time. Many of the fine large gardens photographed for books took decades to complete. The process is part of the pleasure.

53

Create a private spot with a gazebo

Gazebos have an ancient history, dating back five thousand years to the Egyptian royalty who featured them in formal gardens. In Persian gardens, they were often placed at the union of four pools, making a treasured spot for daily meditation. The fifteenth-century English perched theirs on top of garden walls to gain an overview of both the garden and the surrounding countryside. In Colonial America, gazebos were elegant shelters where one could escape from the hot summer sun.

Because of a resurgence in popularity, a wide assortment of gazebos is on the market today. Costs range from small kits priced under four thousand dollars to grand structures selling for tens of thousands of dollars. At either end of the spectrum, a gazebo is a worthwhile investment as a sheltered garden room on a large property.

The gazebo gives a sense of enclosure and protection without blocking the magnificient vistas of the surrounding landscape.

Place a gazebo in a spot where people will want to sit. Here, one is nicely situated at the end of a pond in the shelter of tall trees.

54

Create a private spot with a sheltered bench in a corner of the garden

It's a big world out there, and periodically people need a sequestered spot where they can retreat from the stresses of life. A hidden place to sit in a large garden is especially appealing. It is a place to restore the soul. In a secret garden, wonderful things can happen. At the same time, it gives a delightful sense of mystery and surprise to your landscape.

Finding the right spot is important. Writing in his 1936 book, *Garden Decoration and Ornament*, G. A. Jellicoe said, "The first object of a seat is invitation. Its position should be such that it should attract either because it offers rest at the end of a long walk, or because it is so placed that its surroundings may give rise to pleasant contemplation. The permanent seat should have a suggestion of background because the human being finds it more restful and comforting to have a sense of shelter and to look towards one direction only."

Seemingly perched on the edge of the world, this secluded seating area is the ideal place to escape in the cool of the evening to enjoy the golden light of the setting sun.

Backed by a protecting arc of boxwood shrubs, and looking out into the herb garden, this brick patio is a wonderfully private place to enjoy the scent of sage and the hum of bees.

Children are enchanted by hiding places where they can retreat from the large-scale grown-up world. Here, under the shelter of the multistemmed melaleuca tree (*Alyogyne*), is the perfect spot for a child's tea party or secret meeting.

55

Create a private spot under an arbor or in a covered seating area

Like gazebos, arbors add architectural interest to a garden. They can mark the entrance to a garden room, serve as a transition between two spaces, or be tucked in a corner as a hideaway in the garden. Placed in the right position, an arbor will frame a vista like a picture window. Use the arbor to support a vining plant. Climbing roses are an obvious choice, but also consider wisteria, grape vines, clematis, honeysuckle, sweet peas, or even runner beans.

A covered seating area also assumes a position of importance in the garden, both architecturally and emotionally. It is a haven from the sun and, with a table, may become the favorite place for summertime meals.

Above: This rustic shelter overlooks a large meadow. It's the perfect place to watch the children at play, and to enjoy the daffodils that pop up each spring.

Left: This garden room, with a lath ceiling that admits filtered sun and with leafy walls to enclose it, makes a marvelous room for *al fresco* dining.

56
Divide large spaces into garden rooms

The concept of garden rooms is centuries old. The terraced Italian gardens built in the sixteenth century were a series of rooms that became less formal as they moved farther away from the house. The French adapted the concept to their flat terrain, creating rooms defined by parterres, walls, and paving, linked by *allées* and grand canals.

Across the Channel, the English also planted their gardens as a series of rooms, some of them with plant themes and some of them extremely formal. Still others were carefully planned in terms of layout but informally planted. Phillip Watson, a landscape designer working out of Fredericksburg, Virginia, thinks of garden rooms visually, in terms of vignettes. "In a large garden, I plan lots of vignettes," he says. "I determine the size of the vignette by what you can see in a wide-angle camera lens because that's about how much the eye can take in. The exception is if you have a vantage point high enough or far enough away to take in more."

Stacked pots serve as plinths supporting the urns that mark the entrance to this garden room. On the far side, peaked arbors lead to the spot.

A special doorway to a garden room becomes the threshold of a magical place.

57

Divide large spaces with paths

In addition to providing access from one point to another, a path gives a sense of orderliness and structure to a garden. Depending on your taste and garden philosophy, you may want rigidly straight paths or gently curving and meandering ones. Traditionally, Western gardens have had straight paths designed with a clear geometry. Eastern gardens, especially the stroll gardens of China and Japan, have sinuous, winding paths that encourage the visitor to walk slowly, stopping often to admire a view or a plant. Either way, paths are especially valuable on a large property to lead visitors from one part of the garden to another and to define the space for the viewer.

An island bed of small trees and shrubs surrounded by a lawn path breaks up this large expanse of land.

A path between two large garden beds provides visual breathing space, as well as an opportunity to get closer to the plants.

Being led down the garden path connotes betrayal, but when the garden path meanders through a woodland garden of blooming azaleas and dogwood, the rewards are great.

58

Create visual links between different areas by repeating plants

Repeating plants in several parts of a large garden is like repeating a theme or motif in a symphony. Each time it is recapitulated, the theme is explored and developed in a different setting, providing simultaneous unity and diversity to the composition.

This device is particularly valuable in a large garden to tie diverse elements together. On page 36, the photograph shows a lawn edged with a border of begonias that extends for about 20 feet. The same begonias are planted around the corner in a border along a patio (as shown in the bottom photograph on page 40). The two spaces are very different and cannot be seen at the same time, but in our memory, a visual link is provided by the plantings of similar flowers.

59

Create visual links between different areas by using ground covers

Just as wall-to-wall carpeting or hardwood flooring throughout a home unifies it and gives continuity from room to room, so ground covers can be used in a garden to connect and organize vast spaces. In a large garden, use a ground cover to draw the eye from one space to another, or to lead a visitor from one part of the garden to another.

A river of pachysandra flows through the garden, drawing the eye along its course and linking different parts of this large garden to each other.

This avenue of lawn is interrupted by a statue surrounded by a clipped hedge, but then the avenue continues beyond, creating a connecting link between these two garden spaces.

PROBLEM EIGHT:

An Unsightly View

J ust as an outstanding view can add 30 percent to the value of a property, an unattractive vista can diminish its worth. Fortunately, the art of gardening is not only to take a lovely place and make it even more beautiful; a garden can also transform an ugly setting into something really special. Often when you exercise ingenuity and creativity in solving a landscape problem, the problem becomes an asset.

In the garden, there are lots of ways to hide or disguise an unpleasant view that mars the beauty of the scene or infringes on privacy. Fences and walls, trellises, trees, and shrubs can all work as screens to block an ugly sight, at the same time enhancing your garden setting.

60

Cover a bare wall with plants

A plant that is well chosen and carefully placed can work miracles in transforming a stark, bare wall from an eyesore into a beauty. The solution might be a tree or shrub espaliered in a stylized form, such as the outstretched spans of the horizontal cordon or the vertical palmettes, which begin growing horizontally but then turn straight up at a 90-degree angle. For a carefree look, train lush vines and climbers to grow up a wall, or to cascade down it. Create an architectural feel with shrubs that have multiple woody stems topped with bushy heads. Remove any leaves so that the stems create a bare fretwork design against the wall. Allow the tops of the shrubs to bush out as a soft crown. If your ground space is minimal or nonexistent, put big plants into large pots and grow them next to the wall.

The large, feathery leaves of the tall Australian tree fern (*Cyathea australis*, or *Alsophila australis*) provide relief from this two-story expanse of wall, adding a pleasing contrast of color and texture to the setting.

Climbing roses frame spaces in this salmon-colored wall, creating an interesting pattern that softens the otherwise bare expanse of stucco. The creeping rosemary and other low shrubs perform the same softening function along the base.

Vines for screening

Anemopaegma chamberlaynii, zone 10

Billardiera longiflora, zones 8–10

Black-eyed Susan vine (Thunbergia alata), annual

Bleeding heart vine (Clerodendrum thomsoniae), zone 10

Bokhara fleece flower (Polygonum baldschuanicum), zones 5–9

Bougainvillea, zones 9–10

Bower vine (Pandorea jasminoides), zone 10

Canary Island ivy (Hedera canariensis), zones 9–10

Cape plumbago (Plumbago auriculata), zones 9–10

Carolina jasmine (Gelsemium sempervirens), zones 7–9

Chile vine, coral vine (Berberidopsis corallina) zones 8–9

Clematis, zones 4–9

Climbing hydrangea (Hydrangea anomala), zones 4–9

Clytostoma callistegioides, zone 10

Common English ivy (Hedera helix), zones 5–9

Common white jasmine (Jasminum officinale), zones 9–10

Convolvulus althaeoides, zones 6–8

Coral vine (Antigonon leptopus), zones 8–10

Easter-lily vine (Beaumontia grandiflora), zone 10

Euonymus fortunei, zones 5–9

Everlasting pea (Lathyrus grandiflorus), zones 6–9

Fatshedera (X Fatshedera lizei), zones 7–10

Grape ivy (Cissus rhombifolia), zones 9–10

Hardenbergia comptoniana, zone 10

Hibbertia scandens, zone 10

Honeysuckle (Lonicera), zones 4–10

Jade vine (Strongylodon macrobotrys), zone 10

Japanese creeper (Parthenocissus), zones 5–9

Kadsura japonica, zones 7–9

Kennedia rubicunda, zone 10

Mandeveilla X amabilis 'Alice du Pont', zone 10

Marmalade bush (Streptosolen jamesonii), zones 9–10

Morning glory (Ipomoea purpurea), annual

Pileostegia viburnoides, zones 7–10

Potato vine (Solanum jasminoides), zones 8–10

Primrose jasmine (Jasminum mesnyi), zones 8–10

Rose (Rosa, climbing varieties), hardiness varies

Royal jasmine (Jasminum grandiflorum), zones 9–10

Schisandra rubriflora, zones 8–10

Schizophragma integrifolium, zones 5–9

Star jasmine (Trachelospermum jasminoides), zones 8–10

Sweet pea (Lathyrus odoratus), annual

Nasturtium (Tropaeolum tricolorum), zone 10

Vermilion nasturtium (Tropaeolum speciosum), zones 7–9

Vine grape (Vitis vinifera), zones 6–9

Wisteria, zones 5–10

Yellow-leaved hop (Humulus lupulus 'Aureus'), zones 6–9

61

Use decorative fences and walls

Robert Frost lamented the building of walls and fences in his famous poem "Mending Wall," but in fact, good fences (and walls) can add immeasurably to the beauty and structure of a garden. In situations where the setting behind the wall or fence is unattractive, these structures can be indispensable for blocking them from view.

Budget considerations are important when you decide on the type of wall or fence. Also keep in mind the style and tone of your landscape, and use your creativity to make the structure a pleasing architectural asset to the garden.

Walls and fences can be combined to good effect. Here, the low wall is given added height by the picket fence running along the top. The fence gives added visual interest and increases privacy without the need for a tall, looming wall of oppressive height.

A simple rustic fence has a extra charm in the proper setting, especially when it is enhanced by a vining plant such as this white-flowered *Clematis montana*. Notice that the rocks along the fence line have been left standing in their place, and the fence has been built over them.

Ameliorate the starkness of an adobe or cement wall with structural detailing such as the small buttresses that flank this planter.

The trellis work topping this fence is a pleasing decorative feature and gives added height without making the fence feel too tall and imposing.

Plants for hedges

TREES

Brush cherry eugenia (*Syzygium paniculatum*), zones 9–10

Hawthorn (*Crataegus monogyna*), zones 4–7

Holly (*Ilex*), hardiness varies

Hornbeam (*Carpinus betulus* 'Fastigiata'), zones 5–9

Pittosporum species, zones 8–10

Podocarpus, zones 8–10

Russian olive (*Elaeagnus angustifolia*), zones 2–9

Weeping fig (*Ficus benjamina*), zone 10

CONIFERS

Canada hemlock (*Tsuga canadensis*), zones 4–8

Douglas fir (*Pseudotsuga menziesii* var. *glauca*), zones 5–7

English yew (*Taxus baccata*), zones 6–7

European larch (*Larix decidua*), zones 3–6

False cypress (*Chamaecyparis lawsoniana*), zones 9–10

Juniper (*Juniperus communis*), zones 3–7

Leyland cypress (x *Cupressocyparis leylandii*), zones 6–9

Pine (*Pinus* species), zones 4–10

Spruce (*Picea omorika*), zones 5–8

SHRUBS

Abelia x *grandiflora*, zones 6–9

Box (*Buxus*), hardiness varies

Box honeysuckle (*Lonicera nitida*), zones 7–9

California privet (*Ligustrum ovalifolium*), zones 6–10

Common camellia (*Camellia japonica*), zones 7–10

Darwin barberry (*Berberis darwinii*), zones 7–9

Eugenia uniflora, zones 9–10

Fragrant olive (*Osmanthus fragrans*), zones 9–10

Holly-leaf osmanthus (*Osmanthus heterophyllus*), zones 7–9

Heavenly bamboo (*Nandina domestica*), zones 7–10

Oleander (*Nerium oleander*), zones 8–10

Photinia x *fraseri* 'Birmingham', zones 7–10

Portugal laurel (*Prunus lusitanica*), zones 7–9

Firethorn (*Pyracantha* x *watereri*), zones 6–8

Silk-tassel bush (*Garrya elliptica*), zones 8–10

True myrtle (*Myrtus communis*), zones 9–10

Viburnum species, zones 3–9

Weigela, zones 4–9

ROSES (HARDINESS VARIES)

Rosa californica

Rosa eglanteria

Rosa floribunda

Rosa gallica var. *officinalis*

Rosa moyesii 'Geranium'

Rosa polyantha

Rosa rugosa

GRASSES

Amur silver grass (*Miscanthus sacchariflorus*), zones 5–10

Feather grass (*Stipa gigantea*), zones 5–9

62
Plant rows of shrubs for screening

Plant multiple, staggered rows of shrubs as a useful buffer from low, obtrusive sights. For a formal, unified look, plant masses of a single type of shrub. With skillful planning, you can design a sophisticated combination of plants with different leaf textures and colors. Consider adding golden, red, or purple-leaved varieties of shrubs with variegated foliage. You can also seek out different shades of green. If you like the addition of color, choose flowering shrubs. Plan for a dramatic burst of bloom all at once, or select shrubs that bloom at different times for continual color and interest throughout the growing season.

To further increase your privacy, mound the soil in the bed to create a large berm before you plant the shrubs. Raising the bed increases the height of your shield, and the slope makes the plants in the top back as readily visible as those planted low in front.

The ebullient spray of purple osier (*Salix pur-purea* 'Gracilis') can reach to 5 feet high. A dense plant with a feathery feel toward the tips, it makes an excellent screen. Plant several together to create a hedge.

63

Plant tall ornamental grasses and bamboo for screening

Once newly planted bamboo has taken a year or two to become acclimated, it will shoot up, some of the giant kinds growing several feet a day during the brief growing season. Sizes range from dwarf varieties that can be kept as short as 1 to 2 feet to the clumping giant timber bamboo (*Bambusa oldhamii*), which will grow into 40-foot-tall clumps if not controlled. Bamboo is an ideal screen in areas where there is plenty of room for plants to spread (they can become invasive).

Ornamental grasses are growing in popularity as people recognize their special qualities. Most require very little care, and when properly situated, they are a graceful addition to the landscape. Enjoy the sight and sound of their leaves gently swaying with the breeze, making susurrous sounds as the wind passes through.

A double row of ornamental grasses, the back row taller and coarser-leafed than the fountaining mounds in front, makes an attractive, deep screen. Notice how the sun reflects off the top blades, turning the green shafts silvery white.

64

Grow vines on trellises or chain-link fences to create a screen

Trellising is a wonderful element that is often overlooked as a possibility in garden design. The woven latticework can be as simple as a support for espaliered plants and vines, or as ornate as the fanciful structures, including buildings, arches, tunnels, and seats, that were popular in the design of Renaissance and Baroque gardens.

Because a trellis is, in a sense, a transparent wall, it creates a screen without being too heavy or imposing. Grow vines or climbing plants on it to reduce the transparency, and create a vertical garden. Roses, honeysuckle, ivy, and clematis are traditional choices, but by no means the only possibilities.

The morning glory (*Ipomoea tricolor*) is a fast-growing climbing annual that quickly covers its support structure, and is therefore an ideal plant to hide an ugly chain-link fence. The flowers begin in summer and continue into early autumn. Like the zinnias in the foreground, morning glories require full sun.

A trellis is an elegant yet relatively inexpensive way to define garden rooms or to screen an unwanted view. Here, vining plants grow up the trellis, while pink geraniums cascade down from planter boxes set on top.

65

Plant tall hedges

Tall, dense hedges are an excellent way to block an unwanted view and to define a space. Depending on the shrubs you choose and the way you manage them, the hedge can be loose and informal or meticulously pruned and shaped. Different types of plants can be combined in one hedge to create a tapestry of leaf color and texture, or you can alternate two different-colored flowering shrubs, perhaps red and white azaleas or pink and white camellias, to create a checkerboard effect during blossom time. A dark green hedge, such as yew, holly, or box, makes a wonderful background for other plants, beautifully highlighting a rose garden or perennial flower border.

Chinese holly (*Ilex cornuta*) is a slow-growing plant that, in time, makes a beautiful, rich green hedge. Among many assets, it will grow in almost any soil, and it is heat- and drought-tolerant. Notice that the hedge is pruned slightly wider at the base than at the top, so that light is allowed to reach the entire surface of the plant.

66

Plant tall herbaceous plants for screening

A remarkable number of herbaceous plants grow tall enough to serve as a screen during their season of splendor. Tall varieties of bearded iris grow 27 inches high or more. Other possibilities for tall plants are yarrow (*Achillea filipendulina* 'Gold Plate'), which reaches up to 5 feet; monkshood (*Aconitum bicolor* 'Bressingham Spire'), which sends up blue-and-white flowers on 3-foot spikes; *Astilbe* x *arendsii*, a plant that will grow in semishade with feathery flower plumes as high as 4 feet; blue indigo (*Baptisia australis*), which blooms in spring with lupinelike spires of flowers up to 6 feet tall; and delphinium. Hybrid delphiniums grow from 2 to 8 feet tall.

Although perennials will not make a permanent screen, a tight row of them in full bloom will be a spectacular distraction from an unwanted view behind.

Foxgloves are wonderful, old-fashioned biennial flowers that self-sow easily, so that once they are established, they will return year after year. Native to Europe, the plants grow 3 to 4 feet high; they are a colorful screen during their month-long bloom in late spring. For best results, grow foxgloves in rich, acidic soil in shade or light sun.

Culinary sage is not generally thought of as an ornamental plant, but some sages, such as this clary sage (*Salvia sclarea* var. *turkestaniana*), work beautifully as a floral screen. The tallest of the many sages, reaching as high as 4 to 5 feet, clary is a biennial that blooms only in its second year. Sow seed every year to guarantee flowers each season.

67

Plant rows of trees for high screening

In situations where you need very tall screening, such as for blocking a multistory building or a very close neighbor, trees may be the best option. Depending on the type of tree, the foliage screen may begin low on the trunk or several feet off the ground. Although not often seen in modern home gardens, matched trees planted closely in a row are a striking design element.

If space allows, consider planting a double row of trees along the edge of your property, creating an *allée* reminiscent of the grand French gardens. Ambitious gardeners may want to try weaving the young, supple tree branches together in the center where they intermingle, in a technique called *pleaching*. Walking down a pathway covered by pleached trees that form a living tunnel is a memorable experience.

These tall hemlocks, planted close together, take on the job of screening where the wall leaves off. Two other good choices are Leyland cypress (x *Cupressocyparis leylandii*), which grows at a rate of 3 feet a year to a height of 60 or 70 feet and can be sheared to a variety of shapes, and arborvitae (*Thuja*), which grows up to 60 feet tall.

The heads of these bottlebrush trees (*Callistemon*) have been pruned so they screen the house next door without intruding too much into the pool area. The effect is of a hedge raised several feet off the ground.

PROBLEM NINE:

A Steep Slope

A steep slope dropping off behind or looming up above a garden represents a potential hundreds of square feet of gardening and/or living space that is often virtually wasted. Reclaiming that land to make it useful can be very expensive, but the benefits can make it well worthwhile.

For example, a family in California had a third of an acre of land behind their home, but it was so steep that it was unusable. With the help of a landscape architect, they raised the ground level nine feet at the bottom of the hill, held it in place with a retaining wall, and built a swimming pool in the newly created level space. The rest of the hillside above the pool became the site of a water slide that the children badly wanted (see solution 74), a decided asset. The costs were high, but no more than a major addition to the house would have been, and the family gained far more living space with the garden addition.

If your budget or inclination does not stretch to major garden construction, read on. There are also lots of inexpensive ways to transform a steep slope into a lovely and useful spot.

68

Construct terraced beds with wooden sides

Wooden retaining walls are popular because they are relatively inexpensive and easy to work with. However, because of their limited strength compared to masonry or concrete walls, they generally have to be shorter. Because wood is inclined to rot, use either pressure-treated lumber, or wood that doesn't decay easily, such as heart redwood, cedar, or cypress. The boards may run either horizontally or vertically.

No matter how compacted the soil, no slope is entirely stable. A retaining wall must be able to withstand the enormous pressure of tons of soil. Therefore it is essential to take great care to ensure the structural integrity of the wall. A rule of thumb is to sink the upright support posts in the ground to a depth that is half their length. Each post should be buried in several inches of gravel footing, and the rest of the hole should be topped with concrete. This is a job only for the ambitious do-it-yourselfer or professional.

This extremely steep slope would be virtually unusable were it not for the terracing. Notice the size of the boards holding back the soil. Water-saturated clay soil can produce literally tons of pressure on a retaining wall.

69

Construct terraced beds with concrete, brick, or stone retaining walls

The strongest wall that can be built is a masonry wall made of concrete blocks or of poured concrete reinforced with steel. These are the best choices for tall walls retaining a very steep and/or unstable slope (in regions where there are earth tremors, the structural soundness is vital). Make the concrete surface more attractive by facing it with bricks or stones, or by creating a board texture on the poured concrete.

For shorter walls that require less strength, consider using stone or brick. Stone is particularly handsome and appropriate in regions of the country, such as New England and Pennsylvania, where many of the buildings are constructed of local stone. In the Southwest, people often build walls with stones gathered from a local arroyo.

This brick wall, combined with the brick stairs and paving, is an elegant way to reduce the incline of the slope behind.

Dry-stone walls such as these used to retain the terraced beds are fine as long as they are not too tall and the slope is stable.

Instead of cutting the hillside to create straight, terraced beds, these stone retaining walls are laid along the contours of the slope, stabilizing the soil and creating small, random-shaped planters across the face of the hill.

70

Construct terracing with steps

In a home, a broad, sweeping staircase with shallow risers is the height of elegance. It is possible to create the same special feeling on a steep slope in your garden. The stairs may be very grand, such as those pictured below, or less ostentatious.

For a very effective but less grand look, follow the contour of the slope, digging out wide steps that gradually work their way up the hill. Pave the deep treads with flagstone, leaving gaps for rock garden plants such as small sedums and *Iris cristata*, as well as scented ground covers that can take some foot traffic, such as woolly thyme (*Thymus pseudo-lanuginosus*), creeping thyme (*T. praecox*), or chamomile.

A dramatic split staircase leads up this steep hill to a wide landing. The symmetry of the design is enhanced by the matched pots set at each end of the retaining wall and around the pool, and by the balanced plantings on the hillside on either side of the stairs.

71

Create zigzag paths that traverse the hillside

Zigzag paths cutting back and forth across a hillside make an inexpensive way of gaining access to the garden planted there. Use the same principle as switchbacks on a steep mountain trail to reduce the possibility that the path will be washed away and to ease the climb. If the hillside is densely planted so the path isn't readily visible from above or below, it can be delineated with found materials such as unearthed flat stones, odd pieces of brick or paving, and even the chunks of cement dug up from a building site.

This kind of path is special because it brings you close to the plants, and once you get to the top of the hill, you are rewarded with an unexpected perspective on your home and neighborhood.

72

Construct an amphitheater

For theater lovers, a steep hill offers a marvelous opportunity to construct an amphitheater. Terrace the slope in narrow bands wide enough so you can sit with someone's feet behind you, and with enough drop between the levels for the average seated person to be comfortable. A level space at the bottom, planted with grass or paved, can serve as the stage. Plant the tiered seats with a groundcover that is tough enough to withstand foot traffic, and then plan your theatrical events.

Terraced seats have been carved out of this steep hillside, and grass has been planted on the level sections. Drought-tolerant, low-maintenance ice plant (*Mesembryanthemum*) spills over the top edge and down the face of the risers. The wooden platform built on the leveled surface at the bottom serves as a stage. This garden is the scene of many charity events at which local opera and drama stars perform, as well as of parties at which the guests take part in the entertainment. In addition to the pleasure of the performances onstage, the audience has a panoramic view across a wild canyon to the sea beyond.

73

Create a series of waterfalls on the hillside

The sound of falling water is a magical element in the garden, at once soothing and exciting. You can achieve the effect with a garden fountain or water spilling into a pool or pond, but a steep hill gives an ideal opportunity to create a real waterfall.

The scope for a hillside waterfall design is endless. Orchestrate the sound by guiding the water so that it ripples over pebbles, crashes from a great height, or moves slowly around obstacles in its path, such as rocks or logs. Create slender streams of falling water, known as *silver threads*, or run large volumes of water over a flat ledge to form a "falling-cloth" waterfall. Rainbows form when water droplets hit hard surfaces, splintering them into a fine mist that refracts the sunlight. If your landscape's hillside is quite high, you could create a series of waterfalls,

each of varying heights and different sizes.

In any series of waterfalls and pools, it is essential that the bottom pool be larger than the one on top. Otherwise, when water is taken from it to prime the pump, the water level of the bottom pool will be too low, and when the pump is turned off, the extra water in the lines will flood the too-small bottom pool.

Skillfully placed boulders make this created waterfall look as if it is flowing from a natural mountain spring. The lavender-blooming mounded plants covering the hillside are common aubrieta (*Aubrieta deltoidea*).

Water tumbling over this steep rocky fall makes a dynamic contrast with the still pool of waterlilies below. The stone lantern and the grasslike liriope growing along the bank lend a Japanese air to this garden.

74

Create a water slide on a hillside

Many landscape architects are reluctant to design water slides down a hillside into a pool because of the high risk of failure. Unless the structure is very stable, and the plaster is handled just right when it is laid, the slide is likely to crack. Careful engineering and experienced workers are needed.

"The secret," said Ned Bosworth, the California-based landscape architect who designed the water slide pictured here, "is overengineering." His slide, which is laid on highly compacted soil, is built of concrete with lots of steel reinforcement to prevent differential movement. It has a steel-trowel plaster finish and is sealed with concrete wax.

Working with the plaster is a tricky job. "It can graze [get cracks] if it is over-troweled, or if it is done on too hot a day," said Bosworth. "A cool day is crucial. You also must have experienced workers who can finish fast or the over-worked plaster will get hair-line fractures."

This 22-foot-long water slide drops about 7 feet into the swimming pool. A 2-horsepower pump recirculates the water back up the hill into a retention pool at the top. Notice that the retaining wall of stones rises several inches above the bottom of the slope to keep soil from running off into the pool.

75

Plant a "cottage" garden

A cottage garden is one in which a profusion of flowers of assorted sizes and types live happily together in a haphazard arrangement. Generally the flowers are planted more closely together than is recommended by the nursery, leaving little or no room for weeds to intrude. With a rich soil and plenty of fertilizer, they will thrive.

This charming style of garden is enchanting on a hillside, where the slope gives a clear view of all the plants at once. Create a cottage garden with easy-to-care-for perennials that bloom at different times of the season so that there is continual floral interest. Also consider planting a few dwarf fruit trees and dwarf conifers to add height and structure to the design.

Include a narrow path that traverses the hillside so you will have access to the plants that need care. In dry climates, it is also wise to install a sprinkler or drip irrigation system on the hill before you plant. Water early in the day so that the wet plants won't be damaged by hot midday sun.

Shasta daisies (*Leucanthemum* X *superbum*, syn. *Chrysanthemum* X *superbum*, or *C.maximum*) carpet this hillside in snowy white blooms. These plants do best in cool-summer climates but can adapt to hotter situations if they are given part shade. Most are hardy only to zone 5; however, some varieties will survive colder winters.

Dwarf conifers and small shrubs are a good addition to a hillside cottage garden, giving it a sense of structure and scale, as well as varied texture.

76

Create a cup garden on a hillside

Cup gardens are rather typical of Chinese and Japanese landscapes. They are planted in private, secluded hollows that are formed by surrounding hills or mounds. Often used as quiet resting spots in a large garden space, a cup garden is the perfect setting for a small patio or garden bench and chairs. Whether it is created on a large scale that is governed by a hilly topography or tucked into a tiny space contrived with built-up mounds, a cup garden brings focus to a protected central space, adding a feeling of intimacy. Nothing provides a nicer haven for escaping the world.

Roses, geraniums, and other flowers blend with ornamental grasses in a carefree, pretty combination in this sloped seaside cottage garden.

This private patio, sheltered on one side by the steep slope and on the other by tall shrubs and a wall, is an enchanting cup garden. In keeping with the oriental preference for building gardens full of profound symbolism, the patio is designed to resemble a random-shaped lake, made of asphalt, bordered with a flagstone shore.

Plants for rock gardens

(For additional possibilities, see "Plants for neutral to acid soil" in chapter 5)

TREES

Dwarf pine (*Pinus mugo*), zones 3–7

Japanese maple (*Acer palmatum*), zones 5–8

Japanese red pine (*Pinus densiflora* 'Umbraculifera'), zones 4–7

Eastern white pine (*Pinus strobus* 'Nana'), zones 4–9

SMALL SHRUBS

Azalea, zones 5–9

Ballota pseudodictamnus, zones 7–9

Broom (*Cytisus* x *beanii*), zones 7–8

Crassula sarcocaulis, zones 5–9

Daphne blagayana, zones 7–9

Globularia cordifolia, zones 5–7

Iberis saxatilis, zones 4–8

Jasmine (*Jasminum parkeri*), zones 8–10

Juniper (*Juniperus*), hardiness varies

Polygala chamaebuxus, zones 4–7

Thyme (*Thymus caespititius*), zones 4–7

ANNUALS AND PERENNIALS

Ajuga, zones 3–8

Alpine columbine (*Aquilegia alpina*), zones 4–7

Alpine poppy (*Papaver alpinum*), annual

Alumroot (*Heuchera*), zones 4–8

Alyssum saxatile (syn. *Aurinia saxatilis*), zones 4–7

Armeria juniperifolia, zones 5–7

Aster alpinus, zones 5–7

Barren strawberry (*Waldsteinia ternata*), zones 4–8

Bellflower (*Campanula carpatica*), zones 4–7

Candytuft (*Iberis sempervirens*), zones 5–9

Cheddar pink (*Dianthus gratianopolitanus*), zones 5–8

Cobweb houseleek (*Sempervivum arachnoideum*), zones 5–9

Creeping phlox (*Phlox stolonifera*), zones 4–8

Edelweiss (*Leontopodium alpinum*), zones 4–6

Iris cristata, zones 4–9

Johnny-jump-up (*Viola tricolor*), zones 3–10

Mazus reptans, zones 5–8

Pasque flower (*Pulsatilla vulgaris*), zones 5–7

Phlox subulata, zones 4–9

Polygonatum hookeri, zones 5–9

Prostrate speedwell (*Veronica prostrata*), zones 4–7

Scarlet larkspur (*Delphinium nudicaule*), zones 5–7

Sea pink (*Armeria maritima*), zones 4–7

Sedum kamtschaticum, zones 4–9

Shooting star (*Dodecatheon meadia*), zones 5–7

Trillium rivale, zones 5–8

Viola aetolica, zones 5–7

Wall rock-cress (*Arabis caucasica*), zones 4–8

Wood sorrel (*Oxalis acetosella*), zones 5–8

Yellow stonecrop (*Sedum reflexum*), zones 5–9

77

Plant a rock garden on a hillside

Hillsides are favored locations for rock gardens, perhaps because these gardens were popularized during the Victorian period as environments for the alpine plants that collectors brought home to England from their native mountains. A hillside venue also makes sense because the delicate alpine flowers are easier to see when those planted in back are raised closer to eye level.

Alpine plants do not do well in the hot summers typical of most of North America (the Pacific Northwest is the best region for growing them). However, rock gardens are still popular as an attractive way to highlight small, shallow-rooted plants such as dianthus, *Phlox douglasii* cvs., creeping baby's breath (*Gypsophila repens*), aubrieta, and creeping thyme (*Thymus praecox*).

Although not typically thought of as rock garden plants, cymbidium orchids are an excellent choice because they perform best when root-bound. However, they are practical as full-time outdoor plants only in tropical and subtropical regions of the country where frost is rare. Cymbidiums can take temperatures as low as 28° F., but only for short periods.

The silver-green and rose-colored *Sedum spathulifolium* provides year-round interest in this rock garden, while the bright mounds of spring-blooming *Aubrieta deltoidea* and basket-of-gold (*Aurinia saxatilis*) echo the rounded forms of the lichen-covered rocks.

A sloped rock garden is an ideal place to highlight small, delicate plants. The gravel in this garden is both decorative and functional. It helps keep down the weeds and prevents the soil moisture from evaporating too quickly.

78

Plant low-maintenance plants on a hillside

Because a steep hillside is awkward to get around on, low-maintenance plants are particularly appealing. Look for plants that don't require frequent pruning or deadheading to remove spent flowers, that remain healthy without a regular regimen of spraying for pest and disease control, and that flourish during periods of drought.

Among low-care trees and shrubs are hawthorns (*Crataegus* species), sourwood (*Oxydendrum arboreum*), yews (*Taxus* species), and yuccas. Annuals that self-sow easily are another possibility for a garden that will return each year with little or no help from you. Possibilities are California poppy (*Eschscholzia californica*), cornflower (*Centaurea cyanus*), pansy (*Viola* X *wittrockiana*), snapdragons (*Antirrhinum* species), sweet alyssum (*Lobularia maritima*), and forget-me-not (*Myosotis alpestris*). Perennials that need little care are daffodils, daylilies (*Hemerocallis* species), English lavender (*Lavandula angustifolia*), fern-leaf yarrow (*Achillea filipendulina*), stonecrop (*Sedum spectabile*), and the ornamental grass eulalia (*Miscanthus sinensis*).

This pretty hillside of lavender and gray is landscaped with plants that are quite content to grow on their own without any help. The mounded gray cushion bushes (*Calocephalus brownii*) are at their best when exposed to winds and to salt air and spray. The penstemons, with their tubular flowers, thrive in drought conditions, and the tansy (*Tanacetum amanii*) will also tolerate dry periods.

79

Plant ground cover on a shady hillside

As troublesome as some people find shade to be, there is actually quite a wide range of attractive ground covers that do well in shady conditions and are suited to hillsides. Creeping lilyturf (*Liriope spicata*) is a grasslike evergreen that will grow in sun or shade, tolerates most soils, and will even take salt spray. Dwarf hollygrape (*Mahonia repens*) also grows in sun or shade, as does English ivy (*Hedera helix*) and ground ivy (*Glechoma hederacea*).

Other popular choices for shady locations include Japanese holly (*Ilex crenata*), periwinkles (*Vinca major* and *V. minor*), and *Pachysandra terminalis*.

80

Plant ground cover on a sunny hillside

The ground cover possibilities for sunny locations are many. In zone 10, the most common choices for low maintenance and drought tolerance are the ice plants: red spike (*Cephalophyllum*), sea fig or hottentot fig (*Carpobrotus*), trailing ice plant (*Delosperma*), rosea ice plant (*Drosanthemum*), *Maleophora*, and *Lampranthus*. Also popular is the South African daisy (*Gazania rigens*), which blooms continuously during spring and summer in a brilliant carpet of orange, white, yellow, or bronze. Weeping lantanas (*Lantana sellowiana* and *L. montevidensis*), hardy from zones 8 to 10, are excellent for controlling erosion and bloom twelve months of the year in frost-free areas.

Ground covers for sunny slopes that do well in colder zones include junipers (*Juniperus horizontalis, J. sabina, J. procumbens, J. chinensis,* and *J. conferta*), crown vetch (*Coronilla varia*), daylilies (*Hemerocallis*), dwarf polygonum (*Polygonum cuspidatum* var. *compactum*), germander (*Teucrium chamaedrys*), goldmoss stonecrop (*Sedum acre*), various cotoneasters, and winter creeper (*Euonymus fortunei*). Finally, consider using the species rose *Rosa wichuraiana*, a favorite of influential English landscape designer Gertrude Jekyll, for covering sloping banks.

The uniformly planted gray mounds of lavender cotton (*Santolina chamaecyparissus*) make a striking ground cover on this steep, sunny bank. Santolina looks best if it is kept to 1 foot high with pruning; otherwise it requires little maintenance, growing in any soil and withstanding periods of drought.

PROBLEM TEN:

Too Much Maintenance

The basic principle of low-maintenance landscaping is to select low-care plants, such as shrubs, and plant them in a design that simplifies their care. For example, avoid lots of beds and borders that need weeding and edging. Streamline garden care by grouping plants according to their care requirements. It's easier to fertilize plants in one place than scattered throughout the property. Where you do have beds, mulch generously to keep down weeds and reduce watering (see chapter 1, solution 3). Make paths wide enough to negotiate with wheelbarrows and other tools, and make beds narrow enough to reach across easily.

For patios, walls, and other built features, choose durable materials, such as brick, rather than untreated wood that must be replaced every few years.

Choose tools that simplify and speed up garden chores. Automatic sprinkler systems save hours of time spent watering by hand. Leaf blowers are generally faster than raking, and axe-handle saws make pruning an easier and faster job.

81

Replace part of the lawn with ground covers

A lawn is the most labor-intensive and expensive ground cover available to gardeners. For a presentable lawn, you must mow at least weekly during the height of the growing season, fertilize and possibly spray regularly, aerate, dethatch, and, in dry climates, water.

In contrast, most other ground covers need little or no maintenance once they are established. Some, such as crown vetch (*Coronilla varia*), honeysuckle (*Lonicera japonica*), and germander (*Teucrium chamaedrys*) should be mowed or pruned once or twice a year for the best appearance, but that care is minimal compared to what a lawn requires. As for weeding, a densely growing ground cover should choke out all but the most persistent of troublesome weeds.

In addition to the low-growing creeping plants, such as ivies, ice plants, periwinkles, and pachysandras, that are obvious ground covers, consider plants that can be effectively massed, such as daylilies (which are evergreen in mild climates), lavenders, and ferns. Although not always thought of as ground covers, such plants can do the job admirably.

A dense ground cover, such as this shady bed of evergreen *Epimedium*, will crowd out any intrusive weeds, making maintenance all the easier.

Although some species of oxalis, such as *Oxalis corniculata*, are considered invasive weeds in the western region of North America, others are charming as a ground cover. Pictured here is *O. oregana*, commonly known as redwood sorrel or Oregon oxalis, which prefers part or deep shade in mild-winter climates. Others, such as *O. acetosella* and *O. adenophylla*, are hardy in colder climates.

Combine different ground covers in massed areas to create a subtle tapestry of color and texture.

82

Plant native plants and wildflowers

Plants in the wild do very well without our care because they are well adapted to the local environment. It's the fussy imports that require attention to prevent disease, insect infestation, or damage by temperature modifications and moisture adjustments. If you want a very low-maintenance garden, choose plants indigenous to your region, and

develop a garden design that doesn't require a lot of pruning, edging, weeding, or other general upkeep that will absorb your time and labor.

In the past few years, the concept of wildflower meadows has hooked the imagination of North American gardeners. However, it takes about five years for a newly seeded wildflower meadow to establish itself properly. Meanwhile, it requires a lot of soil preparation (plowing), weeding, and fertilizing. For an instant wildflower meadow garden, look into the recently developed "wildflower carpet." Available at some retailers and through landscape companies, the "carpet" is a

collection of 15 species of well-rooted perennial wildflowers planted in a dense mat similar to grass sod. The mats, which are rectangles measuring about 1½ by 3 feet, are installed much like sod.

Once established, the wildflowers will bloom from spring to fall. At the end of the season, mow the plants to a height of 4 to 6 inches, leaving the cuttings as mulch. The following spring, the plants will renew the cycle.

Native plants arranged in an artistically natural manner can create a very attractive low-maintenance garden. Here in Sun Valley, Idaho, native blooming shrubs and flowers, including columbine, potentilla, and yarrow, make a colorful and inviting floral display that can withstand the dry summers and need little care.

Grouping these native shrubs close together has achieved a lush look that is in stark contrast to the dry hills behind. With just a little irrigation, dry-climate plants will look much greener and fresher than their untended brothers in the wild.

83

Plant flowering shrubs for color and texture

It is a generally acknowledged fact that shrubs require less care than annuals and perennials. However, choosing shrubs to reduce the work in your garden does not mean you have to give up flowers.

Lots of shrubs bear attractive blossoms in their season, and many of them are even suitable for cutting for display indoors.

To create a border or bed of flowering shrubs, work to strike a balance between mass plantings that give a sense of importance to the design and mixing plants to achieve more texture and an extended bloom season. Possible ways to achieve both goals are to plant deep beds with rows of like shrubs, a short variety in front, one of medium height in the middle, and a tall one in back. Space the plants close enough together so that they will grow against each other to fill.

A variety of flowering shrubs, planted in graduated layers, guarantees almost year-round color in this California garden. In spring, the sheared azaleas in front are covered in white blossoms that make the mounds look like snowballs. The middle row of hydrangeas provides summer color, and in wintertime, starting in December and continuing through the spring, the camellia bushes (far left and far right) are perpetually in flower.

84

Plant low-maintenance annuals

To some gardeners the idea of annuals in the garden suggests nothing but work. It's true that they must be planted each year, but many varieties do very well on their own once they are planted, and give almost continual bloom from early summer through to the first killing frost. Among these valuable annuals are impatiens, wax begonia, ageratum (which prefer semishade in all but very cool climates), and the sun worshippers: cosmos, petunia, celosia, annual salvia, dusty miller, zinnia, and marigold. (Both wax begonias and impatiens can be grown as perennials in frost-free climates and will remain in bloom 12 months of the year. When the plants begin to get leggy, cut them back mercilessly. In a few weeks, they will fill out again into beautiful, bushy blooming plants.)

For best results, spend time initially preparing the bed, amending the soil with organic material so that it is friable (crumbles easily in your hand) and adding slow-release fertilizer (see chapter 5).

Ageratum, which grows in semi-shade as well as full sun, is covered in powder-puff blooms from early summer through to fall. Here, ageratums are a dynamic contrast to the yellow marigolds and deep purple verbenas. They also mix well with impatiens and make an excellent border for beds. Protect young ageratum plants from snails.

This mass of marigolds and calendulas took time to plant, but now it provides a spot that needs little care. Weeding is avoided because the plants are packed so closely.

Low-maintenance annuals and perennials

ANNUALS

African marigold (*Tagetes erecta*)

Baby-blue-eyes (*Nemophila menziesii*)

California poppy (*Eschscholzia californica*)

Chinese forget-me-not (*Cynoglossum amabile*)

Cockscomb (*Celosia cristata*)

Cornflower (*Centaurea cyanus*)

Cosmos bipinnatus

Cosmos sulphureus

Flowering tobacco (*Nicotiana alata*)

Forget-me-not (*Myosotis alpestris*)

Gazania rigens

Impatiens wallerana

Livingstone daisy (*Dorotheanus bellidiformis*)

Madagascar periwinkle (*Catharanthus roseus*)

Morning glory (*Ipomoea imperialis*)

Ornamental kale (*Brassica oleracea*)

Petunia X *hybrida*

Pot marigold (*Calendula officinalis*)

Rose moss (*Portulaca grandiflora*)

Sweet alyssum (*Lobularia maritima*)

Snapdragons (*Antirrhinum* species)

Texas pride (*Phlox drummondii*)

Viola cornuta

Zinnia elegans

PERENNIALS

Barren-strawberry (*Waldsteinia fragarioides*), zones 5–8

Blackberry lily (*Belamcanda chinensis*), zones 5–10

Candytuft (*Iberis sempervirens*), zones 3–10

Coneflower (*Rudbeckia*), zones 3–9

Cushion spurge (*Euphorbia epithymoides*), zones 5–9

Daffodils (*Narcissus* species), hardiness varies

Daylilies (*Hemerocallis* species), zones 3–10

English lavender (*Lavandula angustifolia*), zones 6–9

Eulalia (*Miscanthus sinensis*), zones 5–10

European wild ginger (*Asarum europaeum*), zones 4–8

Fern-leaf yarrow (*Achillea filipendulina*), zones 4–8

Hen-and-chicks (*Sempervivum tectorum*), zones 5–9

Japanese anemone (*Anemone* X *hybrida*), zones 6–8

Lamb's-ears (*Stachys byzantina*), zones 4–9

Magic lily (*Lycoris squamigera*), zones 6–10

Periwinkle (*Vinca*), zones 4–9

Sea pink (*Armeria maritima*), zones 4–7

Siberian iris (*Iris siberica*), zones 4–9

Snow-in-summer (*Cerastium tomentosum*), zones 4–7

Stonecrop (*Sedum spectabile*), zones 4–10

Tickseed (*Coreopsis verticillata* 'Moonbeam'), zones 3–10

Wild bleeding heart (*Dicentra eximia*), zones 4–8

85

Plant low-maintenance perennials and bulbs

The beauty of perennials and bulbs is that they pop up year after year, on schedule, with little or no effort on your part. There are some demanding perennials and bulbs; however, many satisfying types require little attention once they are established. Easy-to-care-for perennials include daylilies (*Hemerocallis* species), coreopsis, fern-leaf yarrow (*Achillea filipendulina*), liatris, fringed bleeding heart (*Dicentra eximia*), hen-and-chickens (*Sempervivum tectorum*), stonecrop (*Sedum spectabile* 'Autumn Joy' is a popular hybrid), English lavender (*Lavandula angustifolia*), and lamb's ears (*Stachys byzantina*).

Because the major bulbs (daffodils and tulips) must be planted fairly deep (the larger ones up to 8 inches down), planting them is a big job. To ensure a good, long-term return for your effort, choose varieties that are labeled good naturalizers. These will return vigorously year after year, multiplying and spreading in the process. Among the many daffodils that return perennially are the yellow-and-white 'Ice Follies'; 'Unsurpassable', which resembles the ever-popular 'King Alfred'; the creamy white 'Mount Hood'; and 'Flower Record', which has white petals surrounding a bright orange cup. The species and botanical tulips, such as *Tulipa fosterana*, *T. greigii*, and *T. praestans*, generally come back each spring with more vigor than the fancy hybrids. Protect your bulbs from hungry burrowing animals by surrounding them with chicken wire, or by planting each with a handful of gravel. Sprinkle beds with bulb fertilizer each fall to give bulbs a boost for next spring.

Crocus are easy bulbs to plant because they need to go only about 2 inches deep, and they multiply and come back year after year, as long as the squirrels don't eat them. One variety less susceptible to squirrels is *Crocus tomasinianus*, which comes in pale lavender, rich purple, and reddish purple, depending on the hybrid.

86
Plant ornamental grasses

Ornamental grasses need very little care and look attractive for most of the year. In fact, they are growing rapidly in popularity as people recognize their diverse applications in landscape design and their many winsome qualities.

A sophisticated addition to a floral border, ornamental grasses can create a natural, softening effect along the edge of a pond, or an exuberant statement in a border devoted solely to different grass varieties. Their size ranges from short plants like blue fescue (*Festuca ovina* var. *glauca*) that grow only a few inches high, to major specimen plants such as ravenna grass (*Erianthus ravennae*), which sends up feathery bloom panicles on stalks that reach up to 15 feet tall. Colors vary from bright greens, to blues, and even blood red. Some leaves have horizontal stripes along the blades; others are variegated with more traditional vertical stripes. In winter, many grasses turn a sandy color that accents their striking forms in a stark landscape.

The golden late-afternoon sun glows on the feathery blooms of this mass planting of fountain grass (**Pennisetum alopecuroides**), illuminating the scene and highlighting some of this grass's wonderful qualities.

87
Use hardscape creatively

Hardscape, the landscaper's term for paving and built features in a garden, plays many roles to help reduce work in the garden, and to increase the living space. In mild climates, a paved patio or terrace with suitable furniture is an extension of the house, and even in regions with harsh winters, patios are viable rooms for several months during the summer. Although expensive at the outset, once in place they are virtually cost-free, needing no weeding, fertilizing, mulching, or watering (except for an occasional hosing off). They are splendid borders for beds and lawns, and they add design interest to a garden.

Hardscape materials range from the less-expensive poured cement to flagstone, brick, tile, and exotic imported stone from around the world. Consider your budget as well as the look that will blend best with the style of your house and garden.

A sophisticated study in grays and browns, this southwestern patio is easy on the eyes in a climate of bright, harsh light.

Terra-cotta tile gives a clean, tailored look to this enclosed courtyard garden. The raised planter, built of bricks chosen to match the tile, breaks the monotony of the large, flat surface. Notice the drains along the edge of the planter. It is a simple matter to wash down the paving with a hose and a broom.

88

Design lawn areas to make them easier to maintain

Despite all the benefits of ground covers, there are places in the garden, such as play areas for children, where only a lawn will do. In these situations, design the space to make it as easy to care for as possible.

For example, don't plant the lawn right up against walls or fences. Your mower won't be able to reach the very edge, and you'll have to go back with hand clippers or a weedeater to trim the grass along that strip. Instead, try to have a hard-surface border along the lawn at ground level so the mower wheel can run along that, and the blades will catch every bit of grass.

Trees planted in lawns, although attractive, are also obstacles to mowing and lawn care. In addition, you must rake up the fallen leaves of deciduous trees. Plant trees in beds, where the fallen leaves can be left as mulch, and where they are out of the way of the mower.

In dry climates, invest in an underground sprinkler system with automatic timers. Not only will you save time watering, you'll water more effectively. Set the timer to come on in the early morning so the hot sun won't burn the wet grass, and water deeply and less frequently to encourage deep root growth. Your grass will be healthier and more drought-tolerant.

PROBLEM ELEVEN:

Cool Climate and Short Season

Vegetable hybrids that will grow from seed to maturity in just ninety days revolutionized gardening in regions where the frost-free growing season is just three months long. In these parts of the country, classified by the United States Department of Agriculture as zones 3 and 4, every warm day counts. Even a few days' delay in maturation makes a difference. When hybridizers developed vegetables that matured faster, they gave northern gardeners a wider choice for a short growing season.

Gardeners with a short growing season can cope in other ways besides selecting early varieties. You can find or create warm microclimates in your garden to grow slightly tender plants or to extend the growing season, or get a jump on the growing season by starting seeds indoors before the last frost.

Gardening in northern regions has both challenges and rewards. Someone constrained by the seasons is in tune with the rhythm of nature in a way that a southern California gardener can never be.

89

Place less hardy plants in a protected spot

Most gardens have spots that generally stay marginally warmer than the rest of the property. These microclimates may be created by a walled garden, a south-facing bed with a hedge to break the blast of icy winds, or a brick chimney that absorbs the heat from the sun, and is extra warm when a fire is lit. The difference in temperature in one of these warm spots may not be noticeable to you, but it is to the plants. A warm microclimate in your garden can extend your growing season and make it possible to grow a plant that is borderline hardy in your region.

A famous example of a gardener optimizing a local microclimate is Thomas Jefferson. He planted his vegetable garden on a terrace 1,000 feet long and 80 feet wide, which he had excavated out of a hillside on his estate, Monticello. A massive stone retaining wall, 11 feet high in places, supported the terrace. The entire project is a remarkable feat of earth engineering, but it was worth all the trouble to Jefferson. The slope's south-facing exposure, elevated above lower areas susceptible to spring and fall frosts, allowed him to begin planting early and to continue harvesting longer.

This chimney is a marvelous backdrop for the climbing pyracantha and will radiate heat during the cold winter months.

An enclosed garden that is protected from wind and that gets radiant heat from nearby walls or fences is often warmer than open spaces.

90

Design for winter interest

A well-designed garden should have a definite structure that becomes more evident in winter, when there is less distraction from abundant foliage and flowers. In winter, your hedges, paths, ornaments, furniture, and evergreens—the bones of your garden—stand out in stark contrast to the muted scene. If your garden has good bone structure, it will be beautiful even in winter.

Structures add interest in a garden at any time of year, but especially in deep winter, when they are a welcome focal point in an otherwise bare landscape. Garden benches and chairs serve the same purpose, taking on a new look when they are dusted with snow. Evergreens, especially when pruned into formal shapes, look even more like sculptures in the winter than in summer, and they provide a pleasing contrast to the grays and browns around them. Paths beckon in both summer and winter.

During the summer months (*top*), the evergreen hedge and arbor are mere backdrops to the brilliant blooms of the climbing rose 'Blaze', but when the roses are gone, the arbor and hedge become the focus, an essential design element in the winter landscape (*above*).

The bare white trunks and branches of birch trees are a beautiful garden accent in the winter months. Several birch species are hardy as far north as zone 3.

91
Plant for winter interest

There are many plants that are marvelous during the winter months, adding beauty during a time when all seems dead. Choose trees and shrubs with pretty, colorful bark, such as the red-barked dogwood (*Cornus alba*), an urn-shaped, multistemmed deciduous shrub, or the very cold-hardy birches (such as *Betula papyrifera* and *B. pendula*) with their white bark.

Also consider a plant's shape. Many deciduous trees and shrubs are as interesting or even more so once they lose their leaves to reveal a striking form. Among the plants with arresting winter silhouettes are the twisted Harry Lauder's walking stick (*Corylus avellana* 'Contorta') and weeping willows (*Salix*).

Japanese maples (*Acer palmatum*) are also prized for their bare-branch form, although they are hardy only to zone 5.

Evergreens, especially conifers, give a garden structure and color during the winter months. Berries are another source of color in the winter garden.

Finally, choose a few plants that begin to show signs of life early in spring. Witch hazel (*Hamamelis*) produces flowers on bare branches, with some varieties blooming as early as midwinter.

Chinese witch hazel (*H. mollis*) bursts into fragrant bloom along bare branches in mid- and late winter, introducing a sunshine yellow into the winter landscape.

92
Bring the garden indoors during cold weather

In addition to house plants, consider potting a few of last summer's flowers to bring indoors for the winter. Impatiens, geraniums, and wax begonias will continue to grow and bloom twelve months of the year if they are not subjected to freezes. Certain named varieties of fuchsia, including 'Red Jacket' and 'Angel's Flight', will bloom indoors in midwinter if you root cuttings in early August. Make sure the plant gets twelve to sixteen hours of light each day until it has set buds, and pinch it back every few weeks until the end of October. Allow the soil to dry between waterings, but mist to maintain humidity.

Forcing bulbs is another satisfying way to bring the garden indoors. 'Paperwhite' and 'Tête à Tête' narcissus can bloom indoors within four to six weeks of planting.

93
Protect plants in winter with mulch, burlap, cold frames, and the like

Even many plants that naturally die back in winter cannot take extreme cold because their roots will freeze and die. These can be protected with a thick layer of mulch that will insulate the ground and keep it warmer.

In the northern states and at high elevations, as many plants die from dehydration caused by drying winds as from extreme cold. To protect the plants, spray them with an antidesiccant in early winter, and water them well if rains are scarce before the plants go dormant. Moveable plants should be put in a sheltered spot out of the wind. Others can be wrapped in burlap, which will help them retain moisture.

Cold frames don't give enough protection to keep plants growing through the winter, but they are excellent for getting a head start on the season in spring.

A cold frame doesn't need to be an elaborate glass construction. Clear plastic stapled onto a wooden frame works just as well. Here, the covers are hinged to the planter, so it is easy to open them up on warmer days.

Plants for cold-climate gardens

Ajuga, zones 3–8

Alpine azalea (*Loiseleuria procumbens*), zones 2–5

American hornbeam (*Carpinus caroliniana*), zones 3–9

American white elm (*Ulmus americana*), zones 3–9

Androsace vandellii, zones 4–7

Angelica (*Angelica archangelica*), zones 4–8

Ash (*Sorbus americana, S. decora, S. scopulina*), zones 3–8

Bearberry (*Arctostaphylos uva-ursi*), zones 2–8

Bergenia, zones 3–8

Bird's-foot violet (*Viola pedata*), zones 3–8

Blanket flower (*Gaillardia grandiflora*), zones 4–8

Bog rosemary (*Andromeda polifolia*), zones 2–6

Cattail (*Typha latifolia*), zones 3–10

Cherry (*Prunus pensylvanica, P. tomentosa, P. virginiana*), zones 3–8

Common hackberry (*Celtis occidentalis*), zones 2–9

Daylily (*Hemerocallis*), zones 3–10

Dwarf pine (*Pinus mugo*), zones 3–7

European larch (*Larix decidua*), zones 3–6

Garden groundsel (*Ligularia*), zones 4–8

Gayfeather (*Liatris*), zones 4–9

Horsetail (*Equisetum hyemale*), zones 3–9

Hosta, zones 4–9

Iris species, zones 4–10

Juniper (*Juniperus communis*), zones 3–7

Lady's-mantle (*Alchemilla vulgaris*), zones 3–7

Lingonberry (*Vaccinium vitis-idaea*), zones 2–5

Marsh marigolds (*Caltha palustris*), zones 4–9

Mist flower (*Eupatorium rugosum*), zones 4–9

Phyllodoce x *intermedia*, zones 2–5

Potentilla 'Coronation Triumph', zones 3–8

Red-barked dogwood (*Cornus alba*), zones 2–8

Russian olive (*Elaeagnus angustifolia*), zones 2–9

Scilla bifolia, zones 3–8

Sheepberry (*Viburnum lentago*), zones 3–8

Silver birch (*Betula pendula*), zones 3–8

Spruce (*Picea abies, P. glauca, P. mariana, P. pungens*), zones 3–8

Stag's-horn sumac (*Rhus typhina*), zones 4–10

Stonecrop (*Sedum*), zones 4–10

Thyme (*Thymus*), zones 4–10

Tickseed (*Coreopsis*), zones 4–9

Trumpet honeysuckle (*Lonicera sempervirens*), zones 4–9

Twinflower (*Linnaea borealis*), zones 3–6

Water arum (*Calla palustris*), zones 3–8

White alder (*Alnus incana*), zones 4–7

Wisteria, zones 4–10

Wormwood (*Artemisia absinthium*), zones 4–8

Yarrow (*Achillea*), zones 4–8

Yellowtwig dogwood (*Cornus stolonifera* 'Flaviramea'), zones 2–8

94
Plant a garden of cold-hardy perennials, biennials, and bulbs

The simplest way to deal with a garden in a cold climate is to choose plants that like cold winters. Fortunately, within the fabulous diversity of the plant world, there are many wonderful perennials, biennials, and bulbs that thrive (and in some cases depend) on a long winter chill. Among the popular choices for northern gardens are monkshood (*Aconitum*), bleeding heart (*Dicentra*), campanula, hardy chrysanthemum, coral bells (*Heuchera sanguinea*), daylilies (*Hemerocallis*), delphinium, forget-me-not (*Myosotis*), foxglove (*Digitalis*), ferns, gaillardia, hollyhock (*Alcea rosea*), hostas, Japanese anemone (*Anemone* x *hybrida*), lily-of-the-valley (*Convallaria majalis*), lupine (*Lupinus*), oriental poppy (*Papaver orientale*), phlox, peonies (*Paeonia*), primroses (*Primula*), rudbeckias, vinca, and Virginia bluebell (*Mertensia virginica*). Lilies that do well through the cold are Imperials, Mid-Century hybrids, and Regals. Most tulips require an extended period of intense chill to bloom properly, so people living in northern climates are at an advantage. Other bulbs that do better in cold climates rather than warm are winter aconite (*Eranthis hyemalis*), snowdrops (*Galanthus*), and *Iris reticulata*. These three plants bloom very early, sometimes popping up while snow is still on the ground.

Few plants are as hardy, persistent, and pest- and disease-free as daylilies (*Hemerocallis*). Look for the new hybrids, which are more floriferous and longer blooming than species forms.

Chives (*Allium schoenoprasum*) have a place in both the herb and flower garden. Hardy to zone 3, here their spiky leaves contrast with tansy's feathery foliage (*Tanacetum vulgare* var. *crispum*).

The purple coneflower (*Echinacea purpurea*, syn. *Rudbeckia purpurea*) is a mainstay of summer flower gardens, blooming for several weeks, and ideal for cutting. Japanese beetles may be a pest, but otherwise these perennials need little care.

95

Plant shrubs and trees for cold climates

According to the recent United States Department of Agriculture (USDA) climate zone map, most of the United States is in climate zone 5 or warmer. However, the northern midwestern states, including Wyoming, Montana, the Dakotas, and northern New England are in climate zones 3 and 4, and vast parts of northern Canada are even colder. Even though many plants cannot tolerate these extreme temperatures, there is still a fair selection of lovely shrubs and trees that do well. For best success, check with your local nurseries and your county's cooperative extension office to learn what plants will do best in your specific area.

Among the conifers that can take extremely cold temperatures are the Swiss stone pine (*Pinus cembra*), the Jack pine (*P. banksiana*), *Juniperus virginiana* 'Robusta Green', pyramidal Scotch pine (*Pinus sylvestris* 'Fastigiata'), and the Doumet spruce (*Picea mariana* 'Doumetii').

Peegee hydrangea (*H. paniculata* 'Grandiflora'), purple giant filbert (*Corylus maxima* 'Purpurea'), Tatarian honeysuckle (*Lonicera tatarica*), and red chokeberry (*Aronia arbutifolia*) are considered hardy to zone 4, but may survive in colder areas with protection (see solutions 89 and 93). *Elaeagnus angustifolia*, a deciduous shrub or small tree that produces small, fragrant flowers in early summer that develop into yellow fruits, is hardy to zone 2. So is Ural false spiraea (*Sorbaria sorbifolia*). *Rhus typhina* 'Laciniata' and common sea buckthorn (*Hippophae rhamnoides*) are hardy to zone 3.

Lilacs (*Syringa*) need cold winters to bloom well and so are ideally suited to northern climates. Use one or two as a focal point in the garden, or plant some closely in a row to create a hedge.

96

Plant a garden of annuals

Get a head start on your summer garden by starting annual seed indoors six to ten weeks before your last expected frost. Annuals to start indoors are begonias and impatiens (both of which also can be rooted from cuttings taken the previous fall and kept indoors until spring), ageratum, asters, sweet alyssum, coleus, dahlias, marigolds, petunias, pansies, salvia, and snapdragons. Once the weather has warmed and the plants are big enough to move outside, acclimate them to the outdoors by setting them outside at first for less than an hour, and increasing the amount of time outside daily. This process, called *hardening-off,* takes about a week.

Annual seeds that sprout easily when sown directly in their planting bed include calendula, cosmos, bachelor's button (cornflower), four o'clock, morning glory, nasturtium, Shirley poppy, annual sweet pea, and zinnia.

A bed full of annuals such as these wax begonias, marigolds, ageratums, and sweet alyssums makes an exuberant summer display that will last until the first frost. When you are using so many plants, it is economical to start them from seed.

Zinnias (foreground) are a marvelous summer annual, easy to grow and prolific in flower. Keep picking the flowers throughout the season and enjoy them indoors. The fresh blossoms easily last a week in a vase, and cutting the flowers will make the plants outdoors produce even more blooms. The beds to the left are vibrant with celosia and cosmos.

PROBLEM TWELVE:

Seashore Conditions

Maritime conditions are taxing on plant life. Brisk breezes off the water, sandy soil, and salty air all take their toll on seaside plants. Certain principles for dealing with the seaside habitat apply to both coasts. Wind-sensitive plants (and people) need to be protected. Walls, fences, and rows of trees or tall shrubs are excellent windbreaks, but see solution 98 for an idea that will allow you to block the wind and not the view.

Often, the soil along the coast is sandy, although much of southern California has dense clay. Either amend the deficient soil by adding organic material, or select plants that are adapted to the local conditions. On the southern California coast, drought tolerance is an important consideration. Look at the plant list for plants that do well in seaside conditions (West or East Coast), and notice what grows naturally in your area and what other gardeners are growing with success.

97

Plant a garden of salt-tolerant grasses, flowers, trees, and shrubs

Roses are rewarding, but except for rugosas, not directly on the beach, where the salty air burns and the wind tears their leaves. Some gardeners like to bend nature to their desires, and there is a place for that, but by far the most harmonious and stress-free approach to gardening is to adapt your design and plant materials to the conditions you find. To ensure horticultural success along the coast, choose plants that adapt to the rigorous growing conditions found there.

The best plants for seashore gardens can hold up in strong sun and high winds, are resistant to salt damage, and perform well in soil that is sandy and often dry.

Elymus glaucus, a tough, spreading perennial grass hardy on both the East and West Coasts, is ideal for binding loose seaside soil. A tenacious plant, it is as happy growing out toward the rocky bluffs as inward into the border of gazanias. In the background, you can see a spreading bed of sea fig, also known as Hottentot fig (*Carpobrotus chilensis* and *C. edulis*), a staple in West Coast seaside gardens.

Much of the East Coast shoreline is typified by grass-covered sand dunes. Here bayberry bushes (*Myrica pensylvanica*), which tolerate sandy soil and are native to the eastern United States, make an ideal transition from the wild dune grasses to the cultivated garden. Notice that inside the protection of the bayberries, the soil has been amended so that a wider selection of plants can be grown.

Gazanias make a marvelous perennial carpet in temperate-climate gardens. In the background, the arching blue-gray branches of a large, specimen pride of Madeira (*Echium*) add important structure to the design.

A cottage-style garden planted with catmint (*Nepeta*), iris, *Sedum spectabile* 'Autumn Joy', and ornamental grasses thrives in this sandy soil.

Salt- and wind-tolerant plants

TREES

Australian pine (*Pinus nigra*), zones 5–9

Bay laurel, sweet bay (*Laurus nobilis*), zones 8–10

California pepper-tree (*Schinus molle*), zones 9–10

English holly (*Ilex aquifolium* cvs), zones 7–9

European ash (*Fraxinus excelsior*), zones 5–8

Leyland cypress (X *Cupressocyparis leylandii*), zones 6–9

Mimosa (*Acacia*), zones 8–10

Monterey pine (*Pinus radiata*), zones 7–9

Moreton Bay fig (*Ficus macrophylla*), zone 10

Russian olive (*Elaeagnus angustifolia*), zones 2–9

Sycamore (*Acer pseudoplatanus*), zones 5–8

Tasmanian blue gum (*Eucalyptus globulus*), zones 9–10

White alder (*Alnus incana*), zones 4–7

SHRUBS

Bottlebrush (*Callistemon* species), zones 9–10

Elaeagnus pungens 'Maculata', zones 7–9

Heavenly bamboo (*Nandina domestica*), zones 7–10

Hibiscus rosa-sinensis, zones 9–10

Honeysuckle (*Lonicera nitida*), zones 7–9

Japanese spindle (*Euonymus japonicus*), zones 7–10

Italian buckthorn (*Rhamnus alaternus*), zones 7–9

Natal plum (*Carissa*), zones 9–10

Oleander (*Nerium oleander*), zones 8–10

Pride of Madeira (*Echium fastuosum*), zone 10

Rugosa Rose (*Rosa rugosa*), zones 4–10

Shore juniper (*Juniperus conferta*), zones 6–8

Tamarisk (*Tamarix* species), zones 6–9

Tree mallow (*Lavatera assurgentiflora*), zones 9–10

HERBACEOUS ANNUALS AND PERENNIALS

Aloe arborescens, zone 10

Coreopsis tinctoria, annual

Cornflower (*Centaurea cyanus*), annual

Daylily (*Hemerocallis*), zones 3–10

Farewell-to-spring (*Clarkia amoena*, syn. *Godetia*), annual

Gazania, zones 8–10

Impatiens oliveri, annual

Pot marigold (*Calendula officinalis*), annual

Sea lavender (*Limonium perezii*), annual or zone 10

Sweet alyssum (*Lobularia maritima*), annual

Wormwood (*Artemisia absinthium*), zones 4–8

GRASSES

Prairie cord grass (*Spartinia pectinata* 'Aureo-Marginata'), zones 5–9

Pampas grass (*Cortaderia selloana*), zones 7–10

Ribbon grass (*Phalaris arundinacea* 'Picta'), zones 4–9

98

Use a glass wall for a windbreak

The wind blowing off the sea is stressful for plants—and for people who want to sit outside and enjoy the ocean view. Traditional windbreaks such as fences, walls, rows of shrubs, or trees solve the wind problem but are an obstacle to anyone who wants to look at the sea. A transparent wall made of heavy-duty glass is the ideal solution. Glass walls are generally installed in sections, supported by posts spaced about 10 feet apart, allowing great flexibility in layout and design.

Because glass walls are a see-through block, rather than a solid barricade, it is less essential that the beginning and end merge into something else. You can use just a few panels to create a protected area for sunbathing, or you can run the wall across the entire width of your property.

This glass wall, which follows the curve of the canyon edge, protects the pool area from the cooling coastal winds that blow up the canyon without obstructing the panoramic view.

99

Use driftwood and found objects for ornament

Choose garden ornaments that celebrate the seaside location. Seashells and driftwood are attractive *objets d'art* and even make good containers for shallow-rooted plants. Abalone shells, with their mother-of-pearl lining, are pretty as ashtrays or small dishes. Along the West Coast, lucky beachcombers occasionally find the glass bubbles used as fishing-net weights by Japanese fishers, which have floated across the Pacific Ocean to wash up on the shores of North America. They are useful for ornament as well as conversation. Hang wind chimes from a tree or trellis, and enjoy the music created by the ocean breezes.

In a more formal garden, look for furniture with a shell motif or curves resembling breaking waves. Consider a sculpture with a seaworthy theme. Chipped oyster shells are used for paving paths in eastern gardens, both inland and along the coast.

100

Use a variety of gray, soft-colored plants to ease the glare

On cloudless days, the light along the coast can be hard on the eyes, especially when it reflects off the water. Your garden can be a haven from this glare, as well as a place of cool refreshment, if you plant it with soft-colored, and particularly gray-foliaged, specimens.

Traditionally, gray-green plants have been mixed with pink, purple, and white flowers. The effect is soft, and very pretty. For a bolder look, mix gray or silver foliage with a clean, clear red, such as the brightly colored red salvia.

Among the wide choice of gray and silver plants are silvery yarrow (*Achillea clavennae*, syn. *A. argentea*), artemisia (both *Artemisia arborescens* and *A. schmidtiana* 'Nana' or 'Silver Mound'), dusty miller (*Centaurea cineraria*, syn. *C. candidissima*), bush morning glory (*Convolvulus cneorum*), pinks (*Dianthus*), blue fescue (*Festuca ovina* var. *glauca*), gray-leafed euryops (*Euryops pectinatus*), lavender (*Lavandula*), catmint (*Nepeta* X *faassenii*), woolly cotton (*Santolina chamaecyparissus*), lamb's ears (*Stachys byzantina*), and speedwell (*Veronica incana*). Succulents with gray leaves include bluff or cliff lettuce (*Dudleya farinosa*), hen-and-chicks (*Echeveria elegans*), and stonecrop (*Sedum spathulifolium*).

The splashes of pink and yellow enliven this restful gray garden planted with lamb's ears (*Stachys byzantina*), artemisia, lavender (*Lavandula angustifolia* 'Hidcote'), dracaena, and catmint (*Nepeta*).

Lavender, purple, and pink are traditional colors to mix with gray foliage, creating a soothing garden scene. Here the yellow flowers behind add a lively kick to the whole setting.

101

Use a row of shrubs or tall grasses for a windbreak

In areas where the view is not an issue but the wind is, consider planting shrubs, tall grasses, or even low-branching trees to break the force of breezes or strong prevailing winds. Plants like these make a better windbreak than a solid wall, which can create damaging air patterns as wind passes over them. Plants and open fences slow wind while allowing it to pass through. The poet Robinson Jeffers grew a row of cypress to protect his home and garden in Carmel, California, from the brutal winds off the sea. These he immortalized in his poem "Tor House": "If you should look for this place after a handful of lifetimes:/ Perhaps of my planted forest a few/ May stand yet, dark-leaved Australians or the coast cypress, hagard/ With storm-drift...."

A row of bayberry (*Myrica pensylvanica*) fronted by a dense field of tall grass creates a wind-sheltered microclimate for this waterfront garden.

A backdrop of tall bamboo and ornamental grasses protects this bountiful garden from the ocean breezes.

Index